THE NEW & EVERLASTING COVENANT

THE ESSENCE OF OUR FATHER'S LOVING KINDNESS

THE NEW

&

EVERLASTING
COVENANT

THE ESSENCE OF
OUR FATHER'S
LOVING KINDNESS

JOSHUA SAVAGE

CFI
An imprint of Cedar Fort, Inc.
Springville, Utah

© 2024 Joshua Savage
All rights reserved.

No part of this book may be reproduced in any form whatsoever, whether by graphic, visual, electronic, film, microfilm, tape recording, or any other means, without prior written permission of the publisher, except in the case of brief passages embodied in critical reviews and articles.

This is not an official publication of The Church of Jesus Christ of Latter-day Saints. The opinions and views expressed herein belong solely to the author and do not necessarily represent the opinions or views of Cedar Fort, Inc. Permission for the use of sources, graphics, and photos is also solely the responsibility of the author.

Paperback ISBN 13: 978-1-4621-4854-7
eBook ISBN 13:978-1-4621-4855-4

Published by CFI, an imprint of Cedar Fort, Inc.
2373 W. 700 S., Suite 100, Springville, UT 84663
Distributed by Cedar Fort, Inc., www.cedarfort.com

Library of Congress CONTROL NUMBER: 2024947514

Cover design by Shawnda Craig
Cover design © 2024 Cedar Fort, Inc.
Edited and Typeset by Liz Kazandzhy

Printed in the United States of America

10 9 8 7 6 5 4 3 2 1

Printed on acid-free paper

This book is dedicated to my Heavenly Father, who offers each one of us a path of eternal progression by covenant. It is also dedicated to anyone searching for a closer relationship with their Heavenly Father and is willing to do everything necessary to make such a relationship a reality.

Contents

Acknowledgments. ix

1 The New and Everlasting Covenant. 1

2 The Character of Our Father, the Most High God 7

3 The Promises of the Covenant. 19

4 Jesus Christ and the Plan of the Great God. 43

5 Three Pillars of Eternity. 59

6 The Covenant Relationship 81

7 The Covenant of Love. 109

8 Jesus Christ: The Token of Our Father's Love 127

9 The Holy Ghost: Our Constant Companion. 143

10 Lessons on Revelation 149

Conclusion 165

Appendix: Four Principles of Putting On the Character of Jesus 169

About the Author 174

Acknowledgments

THIS WORK EMERGED OVER A PERIOD OF TIME INSTEAD OF AN IN-
stant, like inspiration often does. When the topic finally surfaced
clearly in my mind, I was intimidated to pursue it because the stakes
felt too high to get it wrong. Hopefully, my best efforts coupled with
the Lord's tender mercies will benefit those who take the leap of faith
and begin reading and who possess the same interest in the topic as I
do, if only in part.

As always, I remain indebted to my wife, Jen, and other early readers of the work who helped improve its content and insight. They include Jane Anderson, P. Jeff Mulitalo, Gail Sears, and Janis Infanger.
Their combined threshing of the work separated the chaff from the
wheat and made it fruitful for prospective readers. The final copy benefited from the fine editorial skills of David Nielsen as well as the fine
professionals at Cedar Fort Publishing. To all involved in bringing the
final copy to market, I extend my gratitude.

Finally, the study of the new and everlasting covenant has done
much to build my faith and trust in my Heavenly Father. It is, after all,
His covenant, His plan of redemption, and His love that created the
initial "swelling motions" of faith within each of us to bring us thus
far. I have come to appreciate more fully His work behind the curtain

of our existence and His constant loving care in bringing to pass the immortality and eternal life of all of us. My love and gratitude for Him have swelled, and I hope it will continue to do so forevermore.

1

THE NEW AND EVERLASTING COVENANT

GROWING UP, THE TERM "NEW AND EVERLASTING COVENANT" WAS not a term I remember being discussed much. Even as an adult, mention of the term still seems a bit sporadic, sprinkled here and there in various general conference messages, Church magazines, and select settings. As a result, my understanding of the term had strong associations with a specific ordinance, like eternal marriage; a particular context, such as the temple; or even a distinct scriptural account, like when the Lord covenanted with Abraham. My discussions with other friends and Church members suggest that I am not alone in my understanding of the term nor in associating it with select situations or occurrences. Does such a narrow understanding of the term matter? Does our linking of the term with the temple or with specific gospel ordinances limit our understanding in some way? Maybe. But seeking answers to these questions is part of the motivation behind this work.

The last leaf of the golden plates from which the Book of Mormon was translated contains what we know as the title page of the Book of Mormon. This page lists two primary purposes of the Book of Mormon: first, "to show unto the remnant of the house of Israel what great things the Lord hath done for their fathers; and *that they may*

1

know the covenants of the Lord, that they are not cast off forever" (emphasis added), and second, "to the convincing of the Jew and Gentile that Jesus is the Christ, the Eternal God, manifesting himself unto all nations." Latter-day Saints often speak of the second purpose—convincing the Jew and Gentile that Jesus is the Christ—but less so of the first, which begs the question: "If it's listed first, should it be—as it was for Moroni—first in *our* advocacy too?" Crossing this chasm requires more from us than what we currently know of "the covenants of the Lord." This book seeks to help us navigate this divide.

The term "new and everlasting covenant" is a term that is understood differently among Christians, including members of The Church of Jesus Christ of Latter-day Saints. A review of the term using an AI search engine reveals that Christians generally believe that the term refers to God's redemptive plan for humanity through Jesus Christ and that it represents the fulfillment of the Old Testament prophecies and the establishment of a new relationship between God and humanity. Under the new covenant, the forgiveness of sins and eternal life are made possible through faith in Jesus Christ and His sacrificial death on the cross. The new covenant of the New Testament is superior to the old covenant found in the Old Testament, which is based on the Mosaic law. The new covenant is characterized by grace, mercy, and the indwelling of the Holy Spirit. It emphasizes the personal relationship between believers and God and the forgiveness of sins through Christ's atoning work.

Across denominations, different Christian sects emphasize different parts of the covenant, such as the externality of God's plan of salvation, or the everlasting effects and implications of the covenant on individual lives and destiny, which influence differences between a sect's beliefs and practices. In short, Christians generally understand the covenant in terms of the grace and love God offers through Jesus Christ. This is definitely an important part of what is meant by the new and everlasting covenant, but it is still lacking. For instance, this view focuses only on the *living* and makes no allowance for those who lived before Christ's birth or for those who have lived and died or now live who have never heard of Jesus Christ, let alone believed in Him. Are they "cast off forever"? According to Moroni, they are not, and a more complete understanding of "the covenants of the Lord" is still needed.

Within The Church of Jesus Christ of Latter-day Saints, reference to the term is multifaceted. For instance, it refers to a personal and profound relationship with God that is not only new but also everlasting in nature. The covenant is understood as a sacred agreement or contract between an individual with God that brings blessings, guidance, and divine promises to those who accept the covenantal terms. The new and everlasting covenant includes faith in Jesus Christ, repentance, and living in accordance with God's commandments. In addition, it encompasses ordinances, covenants, and teachings that are crucial for salvation and exaltation, such as baptism, confirmation, and higher temple ordinances, like the temple endowment, celestial marriage, and other sealing ordinances. Doctrines associated with such ordinances emphasize the concept of the eternal nature of the covenant and its far-reaching consequences. It is seen as the means by which individuals can progress, be sanctified, and ultimately attain exaltation or eternal life in the presence of God along with their families. Such an understanding adds greatly to one's knowledge of "the covenants of the Lord." But at the same time, it carries risks that may emphasize things to do or receive in order to obtain these covenantal blessings.

Latter-day Saints are often criticized by fellow Christians for unintentionally signaling that our works save us—something with which Latter-day Saints ardently disagree. Is it possible that our fragmented understanding of the new and everlasting covenant or our tendency to associate the term solely with a particular ordinance or setting contributes to this misunderstanding? Possibly. If so, this book also aims to help correct this error such that "the covenants of the Lord" can find their proper place in our minds and hearts amidst our daily chores of discipleship.

Reviewing the scriptures and the teachings of modern prophets, several themes emerge about the new and everlasting covenant. First, it is deeply rooted in the nature and character of our Heavenly Father. It is His nature that provides the rationale for the covenant and the motivation for offering it to each of us. All of the promised blessings of the covenant are best understood in the context of our Father's personality and temperament.

Second, Jesus Christ—His life and mission—is central to securing for us the eternal promises the covenant offers and for underwriting the cost of our developmental experiences in the second estate. Without Jesus, the covenant would be impossible to execute between God and humanity.

Third, three eternal events of infinite importance are foundational to the covenant: the Creation of this world and all things in it; the Fall of Adam and Eve, and the Atonement of Jesus Christ. These events, called "the pillars of eternity," are divine pivot points around which all elements of our Heavenly Father's plan orbit and through which His covenant operates. Each of our destinies is eternally linked to these three pillars.

Fourth, the new and everlasting covenant carries a variety of associations, vows, debts, and promises that can be understood in three general categories: conditions, obligations, and ordinances. Understanding the individual and collective effect of this restorative package is essential in providing the personal motivation to keep our part of the covenant.

Fifth, the covenant is more than a contract of conditions and obligations; it is a covenant of love. As such, it is offered on the most generous of terms to the widest possible audience, and none are excluded. It is an agreement that seeks to connect us to God in a very intimate way, touching the eternal elements of our minds and hearts and making us one with God and with our fellowmen.

Finally, and perhaps most importantly, the covenant is structured such that our knowledge of, and gratitude for, our Heavenly Father can expand. In ways I don't fully comprehend, our Heavenly Father has offered us this covenant so we can develop our relationship with Him more completely. What I now know, more than ever, is that the new and everlasting covenant reveals to us our Heavenly Father in a deeply intimate way. If all other aims of the book fail except this final point, then my efforts here will have been enough.

Each one of us under covenant is obligated to press forward along the path that the new and everlasting covenant outlines. Mercifully, we are provided with the promised companionship of the Holy Ghost to not only complete the journey but to endure it well. With the help of the Holy Ghost, the design of the path will transform us into new creatures, preparing us to possess and receive the promised blessings our Heavenly Father intends for us.

To help reflect and capture any and all inspiration you receive as we learn together, reflection questions are provided at the end of each chapter to summarize what you have learned and felt. I have also chosen to let prophets speak for themselves as contained in the scriptures. If you are like me, there is a tendency to gloss over scriptural references when reading a book like this one, thinking, "I have already read or know this part," and only pay attention to the parts that seem "new." If this is your tendency, please do not do this. Instead, read the scripture passages through the lens of the new and everlasting covenant, and I promise you that many scriptural passages will take on new meaning—at least that has been my experience. Through the use of the reflection questions and scriptures, my hope is that you will gain an increased ability to better articulate the new and everlasting covenant to anyone you feel inspired to share it with. In this way, Moroni's injunction will find further fulfillment—"that they may know the covenants of the Lord and that they are not cast off forever."

2

THE CHARACTER OF OUR FATHER, THE MOST HIGH GOD

Our study of the new and everlasting covenant begins with a review of the scriptures. Indeed, the scriptures are the record of the covenant dealings between God and His spirit children. We begin by examining the name "new and everlasting covenant." What does it mean or imply? Our first look at the scriptures for the term reveals that the new and everlasting covenant is both old and new. We usually think of *new* as meaning something of improved quality compared to something currently owned, like when we say, "I need a new pair of shoes."

The scriptures definitely speak of the new and everlasting covenant in this way, and it is in this manner most of Christendom understands the term: a new covenant of improved quality as compared to the old, or Mosaic, covenant. The Lord speaks of the new and everlasting covenant in this sense when He states, "Behold, I say unto you that all old covenants have I caused to be done away in this thing; and this is a new and an everlasting covenant, even that which was from the beginning" (Doctrine and Covenants 22:1). Notice that the covenant is replacing something else and is of improved quality. But the covenant is not "newly created" per se; it is merely being reinstated, "even that

7

which was from the beginning." In this sense, the term *new* in the new and everlasting covenant is functioning as an adjective, in that it is "coming or occurring afresh" to the world.[1] In definitional terms, understanding that the new and everlasting covenant is old leads us to a few questions, such as "How old is it?" "When was it originated?" and "Who originated it?"

The scriptures are clear that it was God, our Heavenly Father, who originated the new and everlasting covenant and that it was initiated before the Creation of the world. Moses refers to one of the activities of this event when speaking to the children of Israel, asking them to "remember the days of old . . . *when the Most High divided to the nations their inheritance*, when he separated the sons of Adam, he set the bounds of the people according to the number of the children of Israel. For *the Lord's portion is his people;* Jacob is the lot of his inheritance" (Deuteronomy 32:7–9). We know that it is our Heavenly Father who is "dividing the nations" because in the original Hebrew, these verses refer to two separate Gods. The first is the Most High— or El-Elyon—who is our Heavenly Father, the creator of our spirits. The second is referred to by the King James translators as the Lord or Jehovah, the premortal Jesus Christ. We know that we are in a pre-Creation context because Moses is indicating that the Most High divided the nations their inheritances and designated Israel as the Lord's inheritance *already*. Keep in mind that Moses and the children of Israel were not yet in the promised land. They had not yet realized or received the inheritance Moses is describing, even that which was foreordained before Creation.

A second scriptural example of the pre-Creation Most High God acting as the originator of the new and everlasting covenant comes from the book of Revelation in the New Testament. In Revelation 5:1 we read, "In the right hand of him that sat on the throne a book written within and on the backside, sealed with seven seals." We understand "he who sat on the throne" to be El-Elyon, the Most High God, and the book or scroll to represent "the revealed will, mysteries, and the works of God; the hidden things of his economy concerning this

---

1. *Dictionary.com*, s.v. "new," accessed August 6, 2024, https://www.dictionary.com/browse/new.

CHAPTER 2: THE CHARACTER OF OUR FATHER, THE MOST HIGH GOD

earth during the seven thousand years of its continuance, or its temporal existence" (Doctrine and Covenants 77:6). And God is in council with every known creature in heaven—men, women, angels, beasts, and so on—presenting a plan to initiate Creation. We know that "[he] who sat on the throne" is different from the Lord, or Jehovah, because we see Jehovah as one who is among the council, stepping forth to take the book out of the hand of "him who sat on the throne." And we know it is pre-Creation because the entire focus of the council is how to initiate Creation.

Each of these examples is illustrative of what we are able to learn from the Bible about the new and everlasting covenant before the creation of the earth. Additional references to the new and everlasting covenant from the scriptures indicate the Most High God's knowledge of our premortal spirits, and they reference a covenant between us—one that involves inheritances, obligations, the times and bounds of our habitation on the earth, and additional future promises all occurring in a premortal setting. For instance, a revelation to Joseph Smith states:

> And also, if there be bounds set to the heavens or to the seas, or to the dry land, or to the sun, moon, or stars—All the times of their revolutions, all the appointed days, months, and years, and all the days of their days, months, and years, and all their glories, laws, and set times, shall be revealed in the days of the dispensation of the fulness of times—*According to that which was ordained in the midst of the Council of the Eternal God of all other gods before this world was.* (Doctrine and Covenants 121:30–32; emphasis added)

The specifics of the covenant as contained in the scriptures, however, are not clear, nor are the motivations of the Most High God in establishing it. More is needed for a fuller picture of the new and everlasting covenant than what we gain from the scriptural perspective alone.

The clearest picture we have of *when* the new and everlasting covenant was initiated by the Most High God, and His motivations for doing so, come from the teachings of Joseph Smith.[2] On April 7,

---

2. See "King Follett Discourse," The Church of Jesus Christ of Latter-day Saints, accessed August 6, 2024, https://www.churchofjesuschrist.org/study/history/

1844—at the funeral of a friend named King Follett who had been killed in a tragic accident—Joseph spoke on the new and everlasting covenant and the motivations of God in initiating it. This was not the first time Joseph had taught these doctrines. Rather, this discourse was the culmination of Joseph's teachings on the subject since at least 1832.[3] According to Joseph, "There is the starting point for us to look to, in order for us to fully understand and be acquainted with the mind, purposes, and decrees of the [Most High God]."[4] The starting point Joseph refers to is the Most High God's character and how His character fuels His relationship with us.

The Character of the Most High God

God's character defines who He is and what motivates His actions. Character is a combination of traits and physical characteristics that determine behavioral tendencies. The character of the Most High God is no different. The scriptures describe the Most High God's physical traits in corporeal terms, meaning He is someone who walks, talks, and converses with men and women on the earth. Indeed, all of humanity is created in the image of the Most High God (Genesis 1:26–27), meaning He possesses a body of "flesh and bones as tangible" as our own (Doctrine and Covenants 130:22), but—and this is a very important distinction—"he is an exalted man, and sits enthroned in yonder heavens."[5] Jesus reiterated this truth to Philip and His Apostles shortly before His death when He said, "Have I been so long time with you, and yet hast thou not known me, Philip? he

---

topics/king-follett-discourse. "The King Follett sermon was the most direct, public explanation" of unique doctrines such as humanity's premortal existence and divine potential.

3. Van Hale, "The Doctrinal Impact of the King Follett Discourse," *Brigham Young University Studies* 18, no. 2 (Winter 1978): 209–225.

4. See Joseph Smith, "The King Follett Discourse," 2, accessed August 6, 2024, https://emp.byui.edu/jexj/new/talks/talks/JS%20KingFollettDiscourse.pdf for an amalgamated version of the text. Note that Joseph uses the term *Great Elohim* in the text, which means the most Supreme God. For consistency in our discussion, I have replaced it with Most High God, or El-Elyon, which is the greatest of the Gods.

5. Joseph Smith, "The King Follett Discourse," 3.

that hath seen me hath seen the Father" (John 14:9). From a physical standpoint, the character of the Most High God is clear: He is a glorified Man of Holiness (Moses 6:57).

Similar to His physical characteristics, the character traits of the Most High God should also be understood by us—meaning the values He embodies that motivate Him to act—in order to know His character fully. Again, the Prophet Joseph helps us understand the situation between us and God "at the starting place." According to him:

- "God himself was once as we are now . . . that he was once a man like us; yea, that God himself, the Father of us all, dwelt on an earth, the same as Jesus Christ himself did."[6]
- God "is a self-existent spirit," meaning that He did not create Himself, but His spirit is comprised of "element, intelligence, or the mind of man" and has existed forever, the same as our own.[7]
- God, "finding himself in the midst of spirits and glory, because he was more intelligent, saw proper to institute laws whereby the rest could have a privilege to advance like himself."[8]
- God offered us the opportunity to "enlarge ourselves," "advance in knowledge," and "be saved in the world of spirits."[9]

What traits does God demonstrate toward us from the first instance? There are several, but here are a few that resonate with me.

First, the Most High God has perfect empathy for each of us. He has known us for a very long time and is familiar with the complete trajectory that preceded our spiritual and mortal life and has accounted for our trajectory into and beyond the world of spirits.

Second, because the core part of our spirits—our intelligences—are co-eternal with God, we must view our creation as a collaborative, persuasive action that honored our ability to choose. Our spirits were not coerced or forced into existence without a say in the matter.

---

6. Joseph Smith, "The King Follett Discourse," 4.

7. Joseph Smith, "The King Follett Discourse," 7.

8. Joseph Smith, "The King Follett Discourse," 8.

9. Joseph Smith, "The King Follett Discourse," 8.

Instead, our spirits were created by God because we agreed to the conditions the Most High offered us. Apparently, our invitation to exercise influence "by persuasion, by long-suffering, by gentleness and meekness, and by love unfeigned; by kindness, and pure knowledge, which shall greatly enlarge the soul without hypocrisy, and without guile" (Doctrine and Covenants 121:41–42) has always been the way things have been done. This should give us pause when reflecting on how we are to lead in our families in the nurture of our own children.

Third, the Most High God saw an opportunity to help lift and bless us—spirits described as "weaker intelligences"—so that we could progress to become as He is. What was in it for Him to do so? Apparently, only the satisfaction of seeing us expand: "For behold, this is my work and my glory—to bring to pass the immortality and eternal life of man" (Moses 1:39), words that embody who God is, not just what He does.

What does this mean in terms of the Most High's motivations in establishing a covenant? It suggests that for a very long time, the Most High God has known us and desired to help us because of His love for us. His character of love, growth, development, and commitment to protecting our freedom to choose has underscored the covenant relationship He offers us. It also suggests that because of our confidence in the Most High God's motivations in lifting us, we were comfortable submitting to the conditions to become His spirit sons and daughters. How this process worked we do not know, but what we do know is that we moved from the original "starting point" as "weaker intelligences" into a relationship with the Most High God where we now call Him Father. "The Family: A Proclamation to the World" states, "All human beings—male and female—are created in the image of God. Each is a beloved spirit son or daughter of heavenly parents, and, as such, each has a divine nature and destiny."[10]

One of our primary motivations to progress through a covenant relationship with our Heavenly Father was His glorified physical body. The Prophet Joseph taught that "the great principle of happiness

---

10. "The Family: A Proclamation to the World," Gospel Library. If this reasoning is correct, our gender would have solidified during this part of our development of the premortal state, for "gender is an essential characteristic of individual premortal, mortal, and eternal identity and purpose."

consists in having a body," and "all beings who have bodies have power over those who have none."[11] Therefore, it was not only our attraction to the relationship as sons and daughters of God that motivated us to act but also our recognition that to receive a glorified body of flesh and bones, we had to first receive a spiritual body in the same likeness.

We do not really appreciate the beauty and grandeur of an exalted man or woman. But for those who have seen them, their testimony is this: Words simply cannot describe what they see. Remember Joseph's description of his vision of the Father and the Son: "I saw two personages *whose brightness and glory are beyond all description*" (Joseph Smith—History 1:17; emphasis added). Or his description of Moroni appearing to him in the upstairs loft of their family cabin: "His whole person *was glorious beyond description*, and his countenance truly like lightning" (Joseph Smith—History 1:32; emphasis added).[12] Our Father's glorified body must have been powerful, persuasive evidence for us to choose to follow Him.

Additionally, the idea that we could so possess a similar tabernacle through our covenant relationship with God would have filled us with all of the necessary motivation to move forward with faith in His promises. Though not a complete picture, enough has been restored to us through these teachings of the Prophet that explain so much about who we are, where we came from, and the role of the Father's covenant in enabling us in our "first instance." The table below summarizes the motivations and promises involved in the new and everlasting covenants from the very beginning, both from God's side and from ours.

---

11. Andrew F. Ehat and Lyndon W. Cook (eds.), *The Words of Joseph Smith: The Contemporary Accounts of the Nauvoo Discourses of the Prophet Joseph* (Salt Lake City, UT: Bookcraft, 1980), 60, from notes dated January 5, 1941, in William Clayton's private book.

12. See also Zebedee Coltrin's description of a vision he had with Joseph Smith and Oliver Cowdery of our first parents, Adam and Eve: "They were the two most beautiful and perfect specimens of mankind he ever saw." "Minutes, 1883 August-December | School of the Prophets Salt Lake City meeting minutes, 1883," 74, accessed August 6, 2024, https://catalog.churchofjesuschrist.org/assets/94111455-7896-451c-8cff-311dfd48c6c6/0/73.

	Motivations	**Promises**
The Most High God	• Love for us • A desire to help us grow and expand • A desire to form a parent-child relationship with us	• The safeguarding of our moral agency • A relationship as His spirit sons and daughters • The creation of a spiritual body as the first step to receiving a glorified physical body
Us as Intelligences	• The Most High God's character and love for us • The Most High God's willingness to protect our moral agency • The ability to obtain a glorified physical body like the Most High God	• Obey the commandments of the Most High God • Honor our relationship as His spirit sons and daughters

Table 1: Initial Promises and Motivations of the New and Everlasting Covenant

DEVELOPING FROM GRACE TO GRACE

It is because of our Father's journey—from where we once were to where He is now—that He is able to share the conditions with us to help us go where He is. The conditions and laws He established to help us advance and expand our development are the new and everlasting covenant. The covenant enables us to come to know Him fully, meaning it provides us with a path to converse with Him, confide in Him, and ultimately meet and dwell with Him in a similar, glorified condition. In short, the covenant provides the path to eternal life, the kind and quality of life that our Heavenly Father enjoys. As Jesus declared, "And this is life eternal, that they might know thee the only true God, and Jesus Christ whom thou hast sent" (John 17:3).

We learn the path of development of our Heavenly Father from the life of Jesus Christ. The scriptures teach that Jesus developed "from grace to grace," stating that "He was in the beginning, before the world was" (Doctrine and Covenants 93:7). Likewise, "he was full of grace and truth," but "he received not the fulness at first, but

CHAPTER 2: THE CHARACTER OF OUR FATHER, THE MOST HIGH GOD

received grace for grace; And he received not of the fulness at first, but continued from grace to grace, until he received a fulness" (Doctrine and Covenants 93:11–13). The developmental process to which our Father, Savior, and we are subjected requires a few conditions to become operational. First, we need someone full of grace to extend to us favor so we can begin our ascent. Grace is the fuel that initiated our development in our life before birth. Second, in order to maintain our trajectory and replenish our momentum, we must give away the grace we receive to another. Thus, we receive grace for grace. Therefore, grace is a principle of reciprocity. One writer explained it this way:

> The extension of favor is meant to obligate the recipient so that he will extend the same. As he meets this condition, more grace is extended to him, which further obligates him to greater assistance of others. Apparently, it was necessary for the Lord to grow through this process. In order to do so, He first received grace, or divine assistance, from the Father. This grace He extended to His brethren. As He did so, He received even more grace. The process continued until He eventually received a fulness of the glory of the Father. The implication of this process is interesting: in a very real way, Christ Himself was saved by grace.[13]

The "grace for grace" principle gives new meaning to Jesus's and our own relationship with our Father. For one, it shows us that to follow the path of Jesus is to follow the Father's path—that our Father is not unfamiliar with the covenant path He has provided for us. In a very literal way, the covenant path is more like a family heirloom, safeguarded and protected by the owner and then vouchsafed to us to use and protect.

Secondly, Jesus taught the Jews, "I speak to the world *those things which I have heard of [my Father]*. . . . I do nothing of myself; but *as my Father hath taught me*, I speak these things. . . . I speak that which *I have seen with my Father*" (John 8:26, 28, 38). Whether as mortal Jesus of Nazareth, premortal Jehovah, or post-mortal Jesus Christ, the Savior never acts unilaterally but always under the direction of His

---

13. Richard D. Draper, "Light, Truth, and Grace: Three Themes of Salvation (D&C 93)," in *Sperry Symposium Classics: The Doctrine and Covenants*, ed. Craig K. Manscill (Provo, UT: BYU Religious Studies Center, 2004), 234–247.

Father who sends Him! (See 3 Nephi 11:11.) As President Jeffrey R. Holland has taught, one of the paramount purposes of Jesus's ministry was to reveal to mortals "what God our Eternal Father is like . . . to reveal and make personal to us the true nature of His Father, our Father in Heaven."[14] Thus, it is essential to see through Jesus's actions His Father's direction and administration of the covenant.

Third, knowing the Father is dependent on knowing the Son first. Because of Jesus's role in the plan of redemption, all knowledge, enlargement, and spiritual expansion from the covenant flow through Him. Jesus taught this principle to His disciples, declaring, "All things are delivered unto me of my Father: and no man knoweth the Son, but the Father; neither knoweth any man the Father, save the Son, and they to whom the Son will reveal himself; they shall see the Father also" (Joseph Smith Translation, Matthew 11:27 [in Matthew 11:27, footnote c]). We are directed in all things toward Jesus because He is the Mediator between God and man, according to divine assignment—or foreordination—in the new and everlasting covenant, which we will discuss further in chapter 4.

Knowing the character of God and His motivations in the first place provides a greater understanding of the covenant He initiated with each of us. It reminds us that the new and everlasting covenant is both new and old, offered to us from the beginning. In effect, the covenant was our beginning! It carries so much potential for growth and personal expansion now. The promises made to us by our Father at "the starting point" must have been attractive and, seeing them personified in the glorified person of the Most High God, surely were compelling for us to choose a fuller life, an eternal life—one where we could secure a better relationship with God than we then had and become His sons and daughters. The fact that we are here now is evidence that we decided the offer was too compelling to refuse. However, entering into a more full and meaningful father-child relationship was not the only thing that made the covenant desirable to us; there were other reasons that persuaded us to act, namely the promises of the covenant. The covenantal promises would motivate us

---

14. Jeffrey R. Holland, "The Grandeur of God," *Ensign* or *Liahona*, Nov. 2003, 70.

to press forward toward the covenant path, which at that point of our existence lay in our distant futures.

Chapter Summary

1. The new and everlasting covenant is both old and new.

   a. It is new because it is newly revealed in our dispensation.

   b. It is old because it was originally offered to us by the Most High God at our "starting point."

   c. The teachings of the Prophet Joseph Smith provide the most detail about God's motivations in extending the new and everlasting covenant to us.

2. The Most High God's character motivated Him to extend the new and everlasting covenant to us.

   a. The Most High God has perfect empathy for us.

   b. He honors our moral agency.

   c. He desires that we grow and develop.

   d. His love for us motivates Him to act on our behalf.

3. We were motivated to choose to covenant with the Most High God at our "starting point."

   a. We trusted He would safeguard our moral agency.

   b. We desired a relationship with Him as spirit sons and daughters.

   c. He promised us a spiritual body as the first step to receiving a glorified physical body.

4. The new and everlasting covenant is a process of eternal development.

   a. Our Father extends grace to us to grow and develop in the covenant.

   b. Jesus's developmental path was like His Father's, the Most High God, within the covenant.

   c. Our developmental path is like that of Christ and the Most High God within the covenant.

Reflection Questions

- What aspects of the new and everlasting covenant stood out to you in this chapter?
- What attributes of our Father's character resonate most with you? Why?
- How has your physical body been a blessing to you? What does it teach you about the Most High God?
- Why do you think it was important to us to enter a relationship with our heavenly parents as their spirit sons and daughters?
- How does the concept of receiving and extending grace affect the way you live your life?
- Who do you know who would benefit from what you have learned?

3

THE PROMISES OF THE COVENANT

INHERITING THE PROMISES OF THE NEW AND EVERLASTING COVE-
nant has always required patience and faith. Even since our premortal
beginning, we have had to grow in patience and faith in our Father's
counsel given to us. Choosing the covenant path to become our
Father's sons and daughters took patience and faith. Faith in what?
That we could become the very spirit children He promised us we
could become.

The decision did not immediately produce the desired outcome
but required faith and obedience after our choice had been made.
Alma alludes to this fact when he teaches us of a priesthood ordination
that occurred for some before Creation. He says they were ordained
"on account of their exceeding faith and good works; *in the first place*
being left to choose good or evil; *therefore they having chosen good,* and
exercising exceedingly great faith, are called with a holy calling, yea,
with that holy calling which was prepared with, and according to, a
preparatory redemption for such" (Alma 13:3; emphasis added).

In chapter 2, we cited some scriptural references to other similar
premortal activities (assignments, inheritances, etc.) that occurred after our faith had been exercised and after we "chose good or evil." We
know very little about our development between "the starting point"

and our becoming spiritual sons and daughters, but we do know a few things: first, it required our freedom to choose; second, it required "exceeding faith and good works"; and third, it was because of those initial choices and obedience to our Father's promises that we received our first assurances of "the immutability of his counsel" (Hebrews 6:17), which would prepare us for what would come later on.

The covenantal promises that motivated us to choose a relationship with our Father in Heaven premortally could only be obtained within the Father-child relationship. As is customary today, certain blessings can only be transferred to a literal heir. These include the genetic blessings from shared parentage as well as blessings that are transferred legally to an heir. The new and everlasting covenant ensures that all promised blessings are transferred to heirs by the eternal laws that govern them. For example, consider these passages:

- "All kingdoms have a law given. . . . *And unto every kingdom is given a law; and unto every law there are certain bounds also and conditions.* All beings who abide not in those conditions are not justified" (Doctrine and Covenants 88:36, 38–39).
- "For all who will have a blessing at my hands *shall abide the law which was appointed for that blessing, and the conditions thereof,* as were instituted from before the foundation of the world. And as pertaining to the new and everlasting covenant, it was instituted for the fulness of my glory; and he that receiveth a fulness thereof *must and shall abide the law*" (Doctrine and Covenants 132:5–6).
- "There is *a law, irrevocably decreed in heaven before the foundations of this world, upon which all blessings are predicated*—And when we obtain any blessing from God, it is by obedience to that law upon which it is predicated" (Doctrine and Covenants 130:20–21).

The promised blessings of the new and everlasting covenant are tied to the laws of the covenant—laws which neither we nor God can change, for they "were decreed in heaven before the foundation of the world." And, as obvious as it may seem, the laws guarding the reception of blessings within the covenant are restricted to heirs, as children of God. This realization is what prompted us to choose, exercise faith, follow God's persuasions, and become spiritual sons and daughters of a Heavenly King!

Accordingly, our Father promises us an inheritance of "all that [He] hath" (Doctrine and Covenants 84:38), but we did not understand such a blessing to be equivalent for each of us. If that were true, in order to be just, we would all have begun with similar gifts and talents, similar faith and obedience, and *remain similar* through the same experiences as we demonstrated our gifts, choices, and desires. Such a monotonous course did not then appeal to the better sensitivities within us. Instead, our Father promised us a path of growth that was unique to each of us—something dependent upon "the degree of intelligence we attain unto" individually, and "if a person [gained] more knowledge and intelligence . . . through [their] diligence and obedience than another, [they would] have so much the advantage in the world to come" (Doctrine and Covenants 130:18–19). Furthermore, the Father ensured us that our heirship would be associated with our "works, according to the desire of [our] hearts" (Doctrine and Covenants 137:9) and proportionate dominions (Doctrine and Covenants 76:111). President Brigham Young explained it this way:

> Improve day by day upon the capital you have. In proportion as we are capacitated to receive, so it is our duty to do. Some learn more and faster than others—more readily see and comprehend the hearings of their lessons and the relationship they sustain to their fellow beings. Then will everyone who secures an exaltation be happy? Yes. Will all be of one mind there? Yes . . . each [will] possess the Spirit of the Lord; and through observing its teachings, everyone will be rewarded and enjoy according to his capacity. Each vessel will be filled to overflowing, and hence all will be equal, in that they are full. Every man and woman will receive to a fulness, *though the quantity will vary according to the extent of their capacity*, and each will be crowned with glory and eternal life, if faithful.[15]

The fulness God promised each of us was to be, ultimately, of our own choosing. All that our Father has to offer us individually will ultimately be determined by the size of the cavity we carve within our

---

15. Brigham Young, in *Journal of Discourses*, 7:7.

eternal spirits to hold, through our own diligence and obedience in fulfilling the terms and conditions of the covenant.

Our choosing of what we become will translate, finally, to the kingdom where we are most comfortable and that best reflects our final natures. Of this principle, President Dallin H. Oaks taught, "We know from modern revelation that 'all kingdoms have a law given' and that the kingdom of glory we receive in the Final Judgment is determined by the laws we choose to follow in our mortal journey. Under that loving plan, there are multiple kingdoms—many mansions—so that all of God's children will inherit a kingdom of glory whose laws they can comfortably 'abide.'"[16]

Possessing and Receiving as an Heir

The blessings of an heir are both possessed and received. Modern usage of the words *possessing* and *receiving* are largely synonymous, so appreciating the differences of use in the scriptures is necessary to determine how the terms are used in relation to the new and everlasting covenant. In the scriptures, the term possessing can refer to a person's physical inheritances, which are owned, controlled, maintained, or used for their and others' benefit. For instance, this is primarily how the term is used in the Bible in reference to inherited lands or material wealth (see Genesis 17:8; Matthew 19:22). Possessing can also refer to traits and attitudes, such as the faculty, attributes, capabilities, or qualities that a person has developed, as when Jesus councils us, "In your patience, possess ye your souls" (Luke 21:19). Therefore, in relation to the new and everlasting covenant, the term *possessing* has reference to the inherited attributes of an heir—an heir with the mental and emotional ability to control the interest of blessings on their own behalf and on behalf of others.[17]

In the scriptures, *receiving* is used in a variety of contexts and can refer to the attitudinal reception of a person's message or presence,

---

16. Dallin H. Oaks, "Kingdoms of Glory," *Liahona*, Nov. 2023, 26–27.

17. I think we should assume that we learned early on, from observing our heavenly parents, that the promises of heirship brought blessings and obligations to bless others. I wonder if it was obvious to us then that to possess their nature—their goodness, love, mercy, and joy—would not only obligate us to do as they have done but would make us want it all the more.

CHAPTER 3: THE PROMISES OF THE COVENANT

willing acceptance of blessings or cursing, and a host of other usages. When it comes to the context of covenantal blessings, however, receiving refers almost exclusively to the rights associated with ownership, including physical inheritances such as land, a crown, a throne, a scepter, robes, seals, and other signs of royalty. Receiving also refers to entitled benefits that come from a predecessor, such as titles, rights of rule, extended familial relationships, and the positional authority associated with such objects. In the new and everlasting covenant, the promise is that the heir may both possess and receive inheritances that internally transform the individual and provide them with the physical resources to rule similar to their predecessors.

One quick point to mention about God's divine perspective. Joseph Smith made it clear that our Father in Heaven does not make distinctions between "time" and "eternity" like we do. According to the Prophet Joseph, "Whatsoever is revealed to us . . . [is] revealed to us in the abstract . . . precisely as though we had no body at all. Revelations which will save our bodies, will save our spirits. . . . When his commandments teach us, it is in view of eternity; for we are looked upon by God as though we are in eternity. God dwells in eternity and does not view things as we do."[18]

God's view of us as eternal beings—versus temporal ones—is important for us to remember because we have a tendency to discuss commandments as if they were temporal. According to Joseph, this is not the case. While it is true that many commandments given to different people at different times were context-specific, such as the command to Noah to "build an ark," all commandments were given to save their souls, not their bodies. In the case of Noah and his family, the commandment had the effect of saving their bodies, but that didn't matter to God because in the long run, there is no final dissolution of the body.

So when the covenant promises heirs to possess and receive in time and eternity, we must acknowledge that even though those under covenant may receive both physical and spiritual blessings that strengthen, sustain, and elevate their performance in mortality, that

---

18. Joseph Smith, "The King Follett Discourse," 9, accessed August 6, 2024, https://emp.byui.edu/jexj/new/talks/talks/JS%20KingFollettDiscourse.pdf.

is not their full intent. As the Lord taught, "All things unto me are spiritual, and not at any time have I given unto you a law which was temporal; neither any man, nor the children of men . . . for my commandments are spiritual; they are not natural nor temporal, neither carnal nor sensual" (Doctrine and Covenants 29:34–35). The promise of possessing and receiving is to elevate their souls to match eternal ruling requirements. In eternity, all elements of the inheritance (spiritual and physical) are magnified, making those who overcome by faith entirely new creatures.

PROMISES OF THE COVENANT

Promises of the covenant go by many different names in the scriptures, with different phrases used to describe the same promise. For example, John the Revelator describes the blessing of the First Resurrection in the negative as "not . . . hurt of the second death" (Revelation 2:11). Peter uses the term "the more sure word of prophecy" (2 Peter 1:19) to describe receiving the assurance of an individual's calling and election, whereas Joseph Smith simply defines it as "a [person] knowing they are sealed up unto eternal life" (Doctrine and Covenants 131:5). Understanding various references to the same promises can be challenging but not impossible. The promises can be mapped to a common set of what I will call "outcome promises," which focus our minds on the blessings we are intended to possess and receive in eternity. There are other promises of the covenant that lift and enable us in our pursuit of outcome promises (spiritual gifts, for example) that we will address later on. For now, our attention is on the outcome promises we stand to inherit as heirs in the covenant, which motivated our faith and obedience from before the foundation of the world.

In my estimation, the most succinct place in the scriptures where the promises of the covenant are mentioned is in the second and third chapters of the book of Revelation in the New Testament. Here, John instructs members of the seven churches, or branches—then anchoring the Church of Christ in the first century—regarding needed behavioral changes to qualify for the promised blessing of the covenant. We know that John is working with promised covenantal blessings because of his introduction to members of the churches in the first six verses of chapter one. This passage acknowledges the purpose for which all of the members of the Church had—and still do—embark; namely, to become "kings and priests unto God and his Father" (Revelation 1:6).

Through John, the Lord reminds members of His Church of the covenantal promises available to each of them. Table 2 (below) lists the covenantal promises organized by those we are to possess and those we are to receive:

Blessings to Possess	Blessings to Receive
• Eating of the tree of life (Revelation 2:7) • Not being hurt by the Second Death (Revelation 2:11) • Eating hidden manna (Revelation 2:17) • Being clothed in white garments (Revelation 3:5)	• Receiving a crown of life (Revelation 2:10) • Receiving a white stone with the name of God and a new name (Revelation 2:17; 3:12) • Receiving kingdoms and a rod (Joseph Smith Translation, Revelation 2:26–27) • Being given the morning star (Revelation 2:28) • Having your name written in the Book of Life (Revelation 3:5) • Becoming a pillar in God's temple (Revelation 3:12) • Sitting with Christ on His throne (Revelation 3:21)

Table 2: Promises of the Covenant

Each of the promises of the covenant is a unique gift, conveying specific rights, powers, authorities, and possessions. Therefore, it is essential to understand how the promises differ from one another to appreciate what each blessing bestows.

BLESSINGS TO POSSESS

EATING OF THE TREE OF LIFE

The first promise we are to possess as an heir is to eat of the fruit of the tree of life. In the ancient world, to eat something was equivalent to partaking of the nature of that thing, to imbibe oneself with the very qualities of the item. Thus, Peter speaks of the precious promises as an avenue of "partaking of the divine nature" of God (2 Peter 1:4). Furthermore, eating is also associated with ordinances that bestow a specific blessing contributive to the divine nature. For instance, both Ezekiel and John ate books, meaning they received an ordinance to fulfill specific actions in mortality (see Ezekiel 3:1–3; Revelation 10:10; Doctrine and Covenants 77:14). We, like them, eat bread and drink water each Sunday during the ordinance of the sacrament to similarly "ingest" a portion of the divine nature and reaffirm our obligations within the covenant (see 3 Nephi 18:3–12).

The tree of life is a consistent symbol throughout the scriptures. It is present at the outset of Creation in the Garden of Eden, referenced in the Psalms (see Psalm 1:3), seen in vision by Lehi and Nephi (see 1 Nephi 8), described as a reward for faith in the Word (see Alma 32:40), and is again referenced in the Revelation of John (see Revelation 2:17). It is a curious tree, one that is guarded by an angel with a flaming sword after Adam and Eve's expulsion from the Garden of Eden (see Genesis 3:24). Nephi was told by the Spirit of the Lord what the tree was—or, more accurately stated, *who* it was. He says:

> And the Spirit said unto me: Believest thou that thy father saw the tree of which he hath spoken?
>
> And I said: Yea, thou knowest that I believe all the words of my father.
>
> And when I had spoken these words, the Spirit cried with a loud voice, saying: Hosanna to the Lord, the Most High God; for he is God over all the earth, yea, even above all. And blessed art thou, Nephi, because *thou believest in the Son of the Most High God*; wherefore, thou shalt behold the things which thou hast desired. (1 Nephi 11:4–6)

Notice the presence of two Gods in this verse, the Most High God and His Son. When asked about Nephi's belief in the tree, the messenger associates the belief of Nephi in the tree with "the Son of the Most High God." And a few moments later, when asked by an angel of the tree's meaning, or its effects, Nephi testified, "Yea, it is the love of God, which sheddeth itself abroad in the hearts of the children of men; wherefore, *it is the most desirable above all things*" (1 Nephi 11:22), "for [the Most High] God so loved the world, that he gave"—or sheddeth—"his only begotten Son" (John 3:16). Nephi indicates here what we all knew at the "starting point" that there was nothing more desirable than the love of God. It was *the thing* "desirable to make one happy" (1 Nephi 8:10), and so we pursued it according to God's covenantal promise.

To eat of the fruit of the tree of life is to have your soul filled "with exceedingly great joy" (1 Nephi 8:12). It is to partake of the divine nature of God and thus imbibe yourself with His love. Such a partaking lies at the end of a strait and narrow path of the everlasting covenant!

NOT BEING HURT BY THE SECOND DEATH

The second death refers to a spiritual death and is a condition of the Spirit based on what we have become during our second estate. It is the condition received by those who did not comply with the conditions to apply the mercy of God to their spirits. It is described in several places in the scriptures (see 2 Nephi 9:8–9; Alma 12:16–17; Helaman 14:18). Modern revelation clarifies that the second death will only apply to a relatively small group of persons called the sons of perdition who will not be resurrected to a condition of glory (see Doctrine and Covenants 76:32–38), or, as the Prophet Jacob calls them, "angels to a devil" (see 2 Nephi 9:9; Jacob 3:11). Modern revelation also contrasts the second death with the covenantal blessing of a glorious resurrection, even a First Resurrection (see Revelation 20:6; Doctrine and Covenants 63:17–18). It is the covenantal blessing of rising in the First Resurrection that should capture our attention, for that is what motivated us to accept the covenant premortally.

What does it mean to rise in the morning of the First Resurrection? It means receiving a resurrection early in the *process of resurrection* after the Savior's Second Coming—a body and spirit that perfectly reflect the laws of the celestial kingdom of God. It is in the Resurrection where all of our passions, weaknesses, physical disabilities, or inequities are rectified—where our physical bodies are made to mirror the state of our spirits. The First Resurrection is an inheritance of a celestial body with a glory consistent with the celestial kingdom. It is offered to all who kept the commandments of the new and everlasting covenant, including those who died without a knowledge of them but would have received them had they known of them in mortality (see 2 Nephi 9:25–26; Moses 15:21–25; Doctrine and Covenants 45:54; 137:7–10). The First Resurrection occurs at the beginning of the Millennium, after the Second Coming of Christ (see Revelation 20:5–6). Adherence to the new and everlasting covenant will be a primary factor in determining the glory that a man or woman will receive in the Resurrection (see Doctrine and Covenants 76:101).

EATING HIDDEN MANNA

Manna was the food miraculously provided to the children of Israel for forty years during their sojourn in the wilderness (Exodus 16:15, 35). Their manna lay on the ground, easy to discover and acquire. Jesus commands us to "labor not for the meat which perisheth, but for that meat which endureth unto everlasting life, which the Son of man shall give unto you: for him hath God the Father sealed" (John 6:27). By meat, Jesus meant life-sustaining food, such as bread, or, in the case of ancient Israel, manna. After Jesus had disclosed that He is "the bread of life" (John 6:48) and directed His hearers, "Whoso eateth my flesh, and drinketh my blood, hath eternal life; and I will raise him up at the last day," He explained, "He that eateth my flesh, and drinketh my blood, *dwelleth in me, and I in him.* As the living Father hath sent me, and I live by the Father: so, *he that eateth me, even he shall live by me.* This is that bread which came down from heaven: not as your fathers did eat manna and are dead: he that eateth of this bread shall live forever" (John 6:54, 56–58).

Therein lies the secret. To eat the flesh and drink the blood of Christ is to partake of His words, regularly and deeply, as a type of feast (see 2 Nephi 31:20). To eat hidden manna is to be filled with God's words—those things that sustain, create, and destroy.

Those under covenant "live by every word that proceeded forth from the mouth of God" with the promise that they will be enlightened by the Father, who "teacheth him of the covenant" (Doctrine and Covenants 84:44, 48). Eating of hidden manna ultimately promises that one may "come unto the Father" and be filled and sustained with "eternal truths from and about God . . . given only to those who

CHAPTER 3: THE PROMISES OF THE COVENANT

diligently seek for them."[19] Thus, the promise of partaking of hidden manna means that those who are worthy will ultimately inherit the capability to rule, govern, and fulfill everything they speak or utter with godly words.

BEING CLOTHED IN WHITE GARMENTS

White symbolizes purity and cleanliness. To have one's garments made white is to have them washed and cleaned completely (see Alma 5:21; 13:11). In the scriptures, white *robes* are worn by both true and false messengers (compare 1 Nephi 8:5 to 1 Nephi 14:19), but white *garments* are only worn by the righteous (see Joseph Smith Translation, Mark 16:3) and are associated with those who have entered into the rest of the Lord, "which rest is the fulness of his glory" (Doctrine and Covenants 84:24; see also 3 Nephi 27:19).

The best description we have of the white garments promised by the covenant is from Joseph Smith in his description of the resurrected personage Moroni. Joseph describes Moroni's clothing as "a loose robe of most exquisite whiteness. It was a whiteness beyond anything earthly I had ever seen; nor do I believe that any earthly thing could be made to appear so exceedingly white and brilliant" (Joseph Smith—History 1:31). Joseph used the word *robe* to describe Moroni's garments, which is also consistent with how white garments are used elsewhere in the scriptures. For instance, Jacob mentions that at the time of the Resurrection, the righteous will receive "the robe of righteousness" and that the robe will be consistent with the receiver's "perfect knowledge of their enjoyment, and their righteousness" (2 Nephi 9:14). Thus, we conclude that to receive the "white garments" is to receive a robe of righteousness at the time of the Resurrection that reflects a cognitive inheritance of complete knowledge of all that we have done well, both in and out of the covenant, and the feeling of satisfaction from such actions. In another sense, as was the case with Moroni's glorious countenance, our whiteness will reflect the glory—or light and truth—we obtained through honoring the covenant.

---

19. Jay A. Parry and Donald W. Parry, *Understanding the Book of Revelation* (Salt Lake City, UT: Deseret Book, 2007), 37. See also Matthew 13:11–12; 1 Timothy 3:16; 1 Nephi 2:16; 10:19; Alma 12:9; Doctrine and Covenants 76:5–7.

Blessings to Receive

Receiving a Crown of Life

Designated members of royalty, specifically kings and queens, wear crowns. Thus, to have a crown is to be a king or queen. To be crowned is to receive glory, honor, and dominion (see Psalm 8:5–6; Doctrine and Covenants 58:4; 75:5), specifically receiving a mansion in the kingdom of the Father. Thus, the crown represents a bequest of a physical place of rule (see Doctrine and Covenants 59:2; 106:8), a kingdom that shall endure eternally (see Doctrine and Covenants 75:5; 81:6). The crown of life is also emblematic of one's righteousness (see 2 Timothy 4:8; Doctrine and Covenants 20:14; 25:15). It is a reward for those who have demonstrated a love of God (see James 1:12), have been willing to serve Him (see 1 Peter 5:2–40), and have given their lives to Him (see Doctrine and Covenants 101:15). The crown is described in appearance as pure gold (see Revelation 4:4; 14:14) and is received after entering into the kingdom of the Father (see Doctrine and Covenants 138:51).

The crown is not an ordinary crown either. It is called the "Crown of Life," meaning it confers eternal lives upon the recipient (see Doctrine and Covenants 138:51), as indicated by the fact that the inherited kingdom is not singular but is described as "many" (Doctrine and Covenants 78:15). It is conferred by "the servants of God" (Doctrine and Covenants 133:32), which suggests that an ordinance is required to ordain one either a king or queen, as was the case in ancient Israel. Furthermore, the Crown of Life confers priesthood power, as was the case with Melchizedek, whose name means "King of Righteousness."[20] Joseph Smith explained, "What was the power of Melchizedek? . . . Those holding the fulness of the Melchizedek Priesthood are kings and priests of the Most High God, holding the keys of power and blessings."[21] Thus, the Crown of Life both confers physical kingdoms—with the authority and power to rule and reign

---

20. Bible Dictionary, "Melchizedek."

21. *The Joseph Smith Papers, Documents, Volume 13: August–December 1843*, 74.

Chapter 3: The Promises of the Covenant

over them eternally—and confers rewards for those who have fully embraced the new and everlasting covenant.

Receiving a White Stone with a New Name Written

Besides the Revelation of John, the white stone is mentioned in only one other place in the standard works, which is in Doctrine and Covenants 130. Here Joseph Smith explains what the white stone is, its purpose, and how it's received: "The white stone mentioned in Revelation 2:17, will become *a Urim and Thummim* to each individual who receives one, *whereby things pertaining to a higher order of kingdoms will be made known*; And a white stone is given to each of those who come into the celestial kingdom, whereon is a new name written, which no man knoweth save he that receiveth it. The new name is the key word" (Doctrine and Covenants 130:7–11)

As Joseph indicated, the white stone becomes a Urim and Thummim to those who receive one for the purpose of learning. "Learn what?" one might ask. The answer: things pertaining to a higher order of kingdoms.

Since the earth in its celestial state becomes a Urim and Thummim to its inhabitants—where everything is known "past, present, and future" pertaining to it and to lesser kingdoms—apparently, more is to be learned by heirs, and the white stone enables the learning process.[22] God has promised heirs of the covenant:

> And to them will I reveal all mysteries, yea, all the hidden mysteries of my kingdom from days of old, and for ages to come, will I make known unto them the good pleasure of my will concerning all things pertaining to my kingdom.
>
> Yea, even the wonders of eternity shall they know, and things to come will I show them, even the things of many generations.

---

22. Joseph Smith also taught, "When you climb up a ladder, you must begin at the bottom, and ascend step by step, until you arrive at the top; and so it is with the principles of the gospel—you must begin with the first and go on until you learn all of the principles of exaltation. But it will be a great while after you have passed through the veil before you will have learned them. It is not all to be comprehended in this world; it will be a great work to learn our salvation and exaltation even beyond the grave." "King Follett Discourse," 5.

And their wisdom shall be great, and their understanding reach to heaven; and before them the wisdom of the wise shall perish, and the understanding of the prudent shall come to naught.

For by my Spirit will I enlighten them, and by my power will I make known unto them the secrets of my will—yea, even those things which eye has not seen, nor ear heard, nor yet entered into the heart of man. (Doctrine and Covenants 76:7–10)

Hence, we suppose that the primary purpose of the white stone is to help us learn additional "principles of exaltation"—lessons about the history of the earth and the future of "things which eye has not seen, nor ear heard, nor yet entered into the heart of man." These things cannot be learned in this world and so are reserved for higher-level coursework for our eternal ascension.

But what of the "new name" written upon the stone? How does it work? Presumably, it unlocks the use of the stone for the possessor "whereby things pertaining to a higher order of kingdoms will be made known" (Doctrine and Covenants 130:10). One also wonders if what is unlocked—or revealed—is unique to the possessor. Perhaps it's a type of customized course schedule—for example, adapted to their knowledge and intelligence (gained by diligence and obedience) in order to realize the promised "advantages in the world to come" (Doctrine and Covenants 130:18–19).[23]

According to a variety of Jewish-Christian traditions, the reception of a new name provided several benefits to the receiver, each of which may apply to the new name written on the white stone. For instance, new names were indicative of degrees—or markers—of one's transformation process. They were given by worthy predecessors, such as patriarchs or matriarchs in the covenant, and conferred power to speak for, or on behalf of, someone else with greater authority. In addition, new names often coincided with a specific mission or commission. Some traditions claimed that new names provided creative powers, including the power to resurrect the dead. Whatever the function or functions the new name will ultimately provide, it is clear

---

23. Truman G. Madsen, "'Putting on the Names': A Jewish-Christian Legacy," in *By Study and Also By Faith, Vol. 1* (Salt Lake City, UT: Deseret Book, 1990), 458–81.

CHAPTER 3: THE PROMISES OF THE COVENANT

that heirs in the covenant will be enabled to know all that is needed of lower kingdoms and continue to grow and expand into kingdoms of a higher order.

RECEIVING KINGDOMS AND A ROD

The covenant promises to provide physical places over which to rule and reign forever. The scriptures describe these kingdoms with gates of "transcendent beauty," with gates "like unto circling flames of fire" and "beautiful streets . . . which had the appearance of being paved with gold" (Doctrine and Covenants 137:2–4). Additionally, the kingdoms "excel in all things" (Doctrine and Covenants 76:92), which suggests that the societal, governmental, and economic systems are much more advanced than what we have currently. Perhaps this is to be expected, as these kingdoms are "given from the Father" (Doctrine and Covenants 50:35) and operate through priesthood channels which "holdeth the key of the mysteries of the kingdom, even the key of the knowledge of God" (Doctrine and Covenants 84:19). In our kingdoms, the knowledge of God will be manifest.

How are heirs to rule their kingdoms? With a rod, which is the "word of God" (see 1 Nephi 11:25; 15:23–24; Joseph Smith Translation, Revelation 2:26–27). A rod is a type of staff or scepter. It abides with the possessor—as the constant companionship of the Holy Ghost—who possesses never-ending knowledge (see Moses 6:61; Doctrine and Covenants 93:24), righteousness, and truth, and it enables one to oversee everlasting dominions, forever and ever, without compulsory means (see Doctrine and Covenants 121:46). The covenant promises real kingdoms, with a very real Comforter, who provides "knowledge of things as they really are and really will be" (Jacob 4:13)!

The first kingdom promised by the covenant to the faithful is the earth, which also receives a crown like unto our own, indicative of it receiving a celestial glory and the presence of our Heavenly Father, the Most High God (see Doctrine and Covenants 88:19). Our Father's covenant to each of us is to restore us to a place already prepared and which eagerly awaits our arrival. In fact, Enoch heard the earth exclaim its desire to be delivered, cleansed, and sanctified (see Moses

7:48).[24] The earth will be renewed, or made new again, having all corruptible things purged from off its face and purified with the light and glory of God. It will become a place fit for our continual habitation and personal development, providing us with everything we need to fulfill the purpose of our creation. When creation fulfills its purpose, we are enabled to fulfill our own.

The purification of the earth is foretold by Malachi, who notes that the earth "shall burn as an oven" and that all corruptible things shall be removed from its face. Only those who have been purified shall "abide the day" (Malachi 4:1). This means that the earth will continue to honor—as God does—covenant keepers by ensuring they are not consumed at the day when it begins its return to His presence.[25]

The new and everlasting covenant is the law that connects our spirit to our bodies in the Resurrection and *connects us with the earth forever.* Through the new and everlasting covenant, resurrected souls worthy of a celestial inheritance are bound to the earth as it transforms from a fallen world into a terrestrial world, then—finally, after the Millennium—into a celestial inheritance. It is the covenant that binds us to the earth, for only those who keep the covenant will have the power to remain during the transformation as the wicked are swept away.

---

24. Unlike most of us, the earth fulfills the measure of its creation by always obeying the commandments of the Lord. "For behold, the dust of the earth moves hither and thither . . . at the command of our great and everlasting God" (Helaman 12:8).

25. "And the redemption of the soul is through him that quickeneth all things, in whose bosom it is decreed that the poor and the meek of the earth shall inherit it. Therefore, it must needs be sanctified from all unrighteousness, that it may be prepared for the celestial glory; For after it hath filled the measure of its creation, it shall be crowned with glory, even with the presence of God the Father; That bodies who are of the celestial kingdom may possess it forever and ever; for, for this intent was it made and created, and for this intent are they sanctified. And they who are not sanctified through the law which I have given unto you, even the law of Christ, must inherit another kingdom, even that of a terrestrial kingdom, or that of a telestial kingdom" (Doctrine and Covenants 88:17–21).

CHAPTER 3: THE PROMISES OF THE COVENANT

BEING GIVEN THE MORNING STAR

Jesus Christ is the "bright and morning star" (Revelation 22:16). Therefore, to be "given the morning star" (Revelation 2:28) is to receive an assurance from the Holy Ghost of "the promise of eternal life" (Doctrine and Covenants 88:3–4).[26] The witness, or knowledge, received from the Holy Ghost of eternal life is also called having one's calling and election made sure. This is because such a witness, in essence, advances the Day of Judgment for the individual. It provides advanced knowledge of the outcome of Judgment Day, providing the knowledge to the individual that their calling and election to rule and reign eternally is assured, or made sure. Their names are written in the Book of Life (as discussed in the next section). Therefore, such information is also known as "the sure word of prophecy" (2 Peter 1:19; Doctrine and Covenants 131:5).[27]

In modern usage, surety often implies certainty in what one knows or believes is true and is often equated with evidence, a guarantee, or a promise. In financial terms, surety is a promise by one party to assume responsibility for the debt obligation of a borrower if that borrower defaults. In this sense, obtaining a surety from the Holy Ghost is the promise that our debts will ultimately and finally be assumed at the Day of Judgment. Having our calling and election made sure is to receive the assurance from God, made in His name, that the recipient will receive eternal life. Through Christ, the sure promise of a better hope was introduced to the world. Through Christ, the surety of a better testament or covenant becomes a reality to the faithful.

Such a witness from the Holy Ghost, who is the first Comforter (see John 14:16–17), carries a promise of a personal visitation from Jesus Christ (the Second Comforter) and God the Father (our Final Comforter) to the recipient (see John 14:21, 23; Doctrine and

---

26. The covenant promises this assurance ultimately to everyone, whether in this life or the next, but such an assurance can be received before one dies as "an earnest expectation" (Ephesians 1:13–14), or a type of down payment and reward for one's diligence and obedience to the covenant.

27. For instances in the scriptures of individuals who received such promises, see Joseph Smith Translation, Genesis 14:25–40; Matthew 17:1–9; 2 Peter 1:16–19; Helaman 10:3–11; Alma 13:17–19; Doctrine and Covenants 88:3–5; 132:49.

Covenants 130:3). The visitation from the Father is attended with "fire and the Holy Ghost" and is protected by a process the scriptures call "becoming as a little child" (3 Nephi 11:35–36), which requires one to adopt the new and everlasting covenant and its requisite virtues (2 Peter 1:3–8). Thus, the covenant requires a person to acquire the nature of God to return to His presence.

The reception of the Second Comforter also conveys access to a special organization in the celestial kingdom called the Church of the Firstborn (see Doctrine and Covenants 88:4–5). Membership in this organization operates in the highest degree of the celestial kingdom, in the "presence of the Father," where heirs "receive the fulness of the Father" (Doctrine and Covenants 76:71), are "[made] equal in power, and in might, and in dominion" (Doctrine and Covenants 76:95), and receive "the privilege of receiving the mysteries of the kingdom of heaven, to have the heavens opened unto them, to commune with the general assembly and church of the Firstborn, and to enjoy the communion and presence of God the Father, and Jesus the mediator of the new covenant" (Doctrine and Covenants 107:19). The Church of the Firstborn is reserved for men and women who have received all of the ordinances of the covenant[28] (see Doctrine and Covenants 131:1–5) and are "begotten through" Jesus Christ (see Doctrine and Covenants 93:22).[29] Getting spirit sons and daughters into the Church of the Firstborn is God's pinnacle achievement. It is the primary purpose of His new and everlasting covenant (see Doctrine and Covenants 77:11).[30]

---

28. A discussion of the ordinances of the new and everlasting covenant is found in chapter 6.

29. A discussion of the role of Jesus Christ as the Mediator of the new covenant is found in chapter 4.

30. It is the primary focus of the adversary, or "dragon," to thwart men and women from entering the Church of the Firstborn at any cost. The Church of Jesus Christ of Latter-day Saints, or kingdom of God on the earth, is likened by John to a woman with child in Revelation 12:1–17. The dragon, or Satan, lies in wait to destroy the child above all else (see Revelation 12:1–17; John 16:21–22).

Chapter 3: The Promises of the Covenant

Having Your Name Written in the Book of Life

The Book of Life is the record of all those redeemed by the new and everlasting covenant. One's name is recorded after the Final Judgment and is accompanied by the reception of fire and the Holy Ghost, which constitutes "the record of the Father and the Son" (Moses 6:66) and is "the record of heaven" (Moses 6:61). When a person's name is recorded in the Book of Life, the recipient is granted an eternal inheritance (see Alma 5:58; Doctrine and Covenants 132:19) according to the works and desires of their heart.

Becoming a Pillar in God's Temple

God's house, or temple, is "a house of order" (Doctrine and Covenants 132:8). The covenant orders things right so that one can enter into God's temple and become a permanent part of it (see Doctrine and Covenants 132:11–12). God's temple is supported by pillars that provide necessary structural support and a "continuation of the works of [our] Father, wherein He glorifies himself" (Doctrine and Covenants 132:31). When an heir receives their inheritance, they "become a pillar in God's temple," or a permanent part of an eternal infrastructure.

The covenant promise is that we can become like "the Most High [who] dwelleth not in temples made with hands" (Acts 17:24) but actually *are* the temple (see Revelation 21:10–21). For instance, Paul taught the Corinthian Saints that the children of the covenant are the temple. "Know ye not that ye are the temple of God, and that the Spirit of God dwelleth in you?" he asked. "If any man defile the temple of God, him shall God destroy; for the temple of God is holy, which temple ye are" (1 Corinthians 3:16–17). And in our day, the Lord has revealed, "The elements are the tabernacle of God; yea, man is the tabernacle of God, even temples" (Doctrine and Covenants 93:35). The kingdom of God on earth is to provide a path for us to grow into the temple of God (see Ephesians 2:19–22).

With the promise of the exalted becoming pillars, what does the temple of God look like? We cannot be sure, but one possibility is a diagram drawn by Orson Hyde in 1847 (see Figure 1 below). He described his drawing as follows:

The diagram shows the order and unity of the kingdom of God. The eternal Father sits at the head, crowned King of Kings and Lord of Lords. Wherever the other lines meet, there sits a king and a Priest unto God, bearing rule, authority, and dominion under the Father. He is one with the Father, because his kingdom is joined to his Father's and becomes part of it [pillar]. . . . It will be seen by the above diagram that there are kingdoms of all sizes an infinite variety to suit all grades of merit and ability. The chosen vessels unto God are the kings and priests that are placed at the head of these kingdoms. . . . While this portion of eternity that we now live in, called time, continues, and while the other portions of eternity that we may hereafter dwell in, continue, those lines in the foregoing diagram, representing kingdoms, will continue to extend and be lengthened out; and thus, the increase of our kingdoms will increase the kingdom of our God.[31]

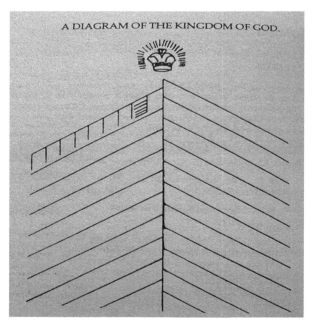

Figure 1: A diagram of the Kingdom of God

Note that each heir will become an intersection within the great and everlasting kingdom of God, providing support to His

---

31. Orson Hyde, "A Diagram of the Kingdom of God," *Millennial Star* 9, no. 15 (1847), 23–24.

CHAPTER 3: THE PROMISES OF THE COVENANT

ever-expanding kingdom as a pillar, with a covenant and promise that we will become a permanent part of his temple "to go no more out" (see Alma 7:25; 34:36; Helaman 3:30; 3 Nephi 28:40).

Furthermore, to become a pillar in God's temple also means to inherit the capacity to eternally expand one's own kingdom. The blessing to increase eternally is fundamental to our Father's covenant with us. We want to become like our heavenly parents, which implies we must receive an inheritance that can continually expand. This aspect of the covenant is perhaps the most commonly mentioned by members of the Church and remains a driving motivation for members to bear children in a chaotic, uncertain, and increasingly wicked world. The promise of an eternal increase has motivated us in the covenant from the beginning and is described as seed, or posterity, that is "innumerable as the stars; or, if ye were to count the sand upon the seashore ye could not number them" (Doctrine and Covenants 132:30).

SITTING WITH CHRIST ON HIS THRONE

A throne is a symbol of divine rule and is a sign of one's claim to power and authority. The promise of the covenant is that we will not only receive a throne but that we will "sit with Christ on his throne" (Revelation 3:21). This means we will be "joint heirs" with Him (Romans 8:17), possessing a legitimate claim to His power and authority, and that we will assume His responsibilities as a savior of men (see Doctrine and Covenants 101:39; 103:9–10).

From our "first beginnings," we have demonstrated faith in our Father's covenant with us. The promises of the covenant motivated us to act, to choose God, and to become something more than we were then. The covenant ensured us that we could be transformed into powerful beings, infinite and eternal, according to our faith, diligence, and obedience. It also assured us of our potential to become like unto our heavenly parents, with power, might, dominion, and exaltation. However, even though we had arrived at the state of spiritual sons and daughters, we knew from the beginning that none of the promises could be transferred alone by our shared genealogy. No, all of the promises were to be contingent upon, and secured through, the fulfillment of the divine plan of the Eternal God.

Chapter Summary

1. Inheriting the promises of the new and everlasting covenant requires patience and faith.

   a. We exercised faith and good works premortally to enter our parent-child relationship with God.

   b. We received assurances from God premortally as we exercised our agency.

2. The parent-child relationship is essential to inheriting the promises of the new and everlasting covenant.

   a. The Father-child relationship entitles us to receive promises as heirs.

   b. The promises of the new and everlasting covenant are linked to the laws of the covenant, which cannot be changed by us or by God.

   c. The promises will be granted according to our capacity to receive and will differ among people.

   d. What we finally receive will be a function of our choices

3. Promised blessings are to be possessed and received.

   a. Possessed promises relate to the character we develop.

   b. Received promises relate to physical inheritances.

   c. Promises are best understood in view of eternity and not mortality.

   d. Outcome promises are described in the scriptures by various names for those we are to possess and those we are to receive.

Reflection Questions

- What aspects of the new and everlasting covenant stood out to you in this chapter?
- What do you feel as you ponder your premortal faith and good works?
- How does your knowledge of your parent-child relationship with heavenly parents influence you today?

CHAPTER 3: THE PROMISES OF THE COVENANT

- How does the knowledge that your diligence and obedience affect your eternal inheritance motivate you today?
- What "outcome promise"—possessed or received promise—motivates your diligence and obedience the most?
- Who do you know who would benefit from what you have learned?

4

JESUS CHRIST AND THE PLAN OF THE GREAT GOD

OUR RELATIONSHIP TO OUR HEAVENLY FATHER AS SPIRIT SONS AND daughters, and our knowledge of the promises of His covenant with us, prompted Him to offer us a path to deepen our covenantal relationship with Him and further our progress to obtain the promises. Our Father sought a forum with His spirit children to present the plan to all of us in a Grand Council. Thus, the initial covenant that brought us into being and into a Father-child relationship was furthered between God and mankind before the foundation of the earth through the Grand Council (see Doctrine and Covenants 22:1).

According to the Prophet Joseph Smith, the first line of Genesis in the Bible indicates that in the beginning, the Head God brought forth the Gods in a Grand Council to present His plan to them.[32] John the

---

32. Andrew F. Ehat and Lyndon W. Cook (eds.), *The Words of Joseph Smith: The Contemporary Accounts of the Nauvoo Discourses of the Prophet Joseph* (Salt Lake City, UT: Bookcraft, 1980), 397, note 70. "The word given here phonetically transliterates from the Hebrew as Re'shiyth (pronounced ray-sheeth). The word, which when transliterated is re'sh, means 'the head' as the prophet applied it here. Joseph Smith claimed the prefix 'Be'— (of Bere'shiyth)—was not required. While in fact, the Dagesh in the bosom of the letter Beyth that

43

The New and Everlasting Covenant

Revelator gives the best view of what unfolded. In Revelation 5, John sees the Lord God Almighty holding a book, or scroll, sealed with seven seals (see Revelation 5:1). To Joseph Smith, the Lord revealed the meaning of the book as containing "the revealed will, mysteries, and the works of God; the hidden things of his economy concerning this earth during the seven thousand years of its continuance, or its temporal existence," where each seal "contains the things of the first thousand years, and the second also of the second thousand years, and so on until the seventh" (Doctrine and Covenants 77:6–7). In other words, our Father was presenting a plan to each of us that involved the Creation of an earth where we could be sent to receive a mortal body and learn how to apply the laws of the covenant through additional experience and training. Abraham provided a glimpse into this event, recording the following:

> Now the Lord had shown unto me, Abraham, the intelligences that were organized before the world was. . . .
>
> And God saw these souls that they were good, and he stood in the midst of them, and he said: These I will make my rulers; for he stood among those that were spirits, and he saw that they were good. . . .
>
> And there stood one among them that was like unto God, and he said unto those who were with him: We will go down, for there is space there, and we will take of these materials, and we will make an earth whereon these may dwell;
>
> And we will prove them herewith, to see if they will do all things whatsoever the Lord their God shall command them;
>
> And they who keep their first estate shall be added upon; and they who keep not their first estate shall not have glory in the same kingdom with those who keep their first estate; and they who keep their second estate shall have glory added upon their heads for ever and ever. (Abraham 3:22–26)

---

begins Genesis 1:1 removes the aspiration of the first vowel, the Prophet says the B (meaning 'in, by, through and everything else') should also be dropped. If this is followed, then he is free to form a translation "The Head one of the Gods organized the heaven and the earth" which comes from 're' shiyth/bara/ elohiym/eth/hashamayim/v'eth/ha'arts.'"

Each of us was presented with a path to the promises of the covenant through an earthly experience where our faith and obedience could be tested in the covenant "to see if [we] will do all things whatsoever the Lord [our] God shall command [us]." However, there was an apparent problem in the Council that none of us knew how to rectify. It involved how to initiate the plan.

The plan of our Father could only be initiated by someone with sufficient worthiness. Among the hosts of His spirit children present, no one seemed to possess enough of it. John writes that the problem was explained to us as follows:

> And I saw a strong angel proclaiming with a loud voice, who is worthy to open the book, and to loose the seals thereof?
>
> And no man in heaven, nor in earth, neither under the earth, was able to open the book, neither to look thereon.
>
> And I wept much, because no man was found worthy to open and to read the book, neither to look thereon. (Revelation 5:2–4)

Apparently, there was a moment of great alarm in the Grand Council, where the collective belief of our Father's spirit sons and daughters—billions and billions of them—was that nobody "in heaven, nor in earth, neither under the earth, was able to open the book, neither to look thereon." In other words, the task of initiating the Father's plan was too daunting because it would require someone to voluntarily submit their will completely to the Father's will "in all things from the beginning" (3 Nephi 11:11) while in mortality and assume an "infinite and eternal" debt as payment for all of the mistakes we knew we would make (see Alma 34:9–10). Ultimately, the plan would require that person to die "for the sins of the world" (3 Nephi 11:14; Doctrine and Covenants 35:2), as explained by the Father in the Grand Council.[33]

---

33. Jesus knew what He was signing up for; apparently, He, like us, heard the Father describe the situation in the Council as the plan was presented. "The great Jehovah contemplated the whole of the events connected with the earth, pertaining to the plan of salvation, before it rolled into existence, or ever 'the morning stars sang together' for joy; . . . He knew of the fall of Adam, the iniquities of the antediluvians, of the depth of iniquity that would be connected with the human family, their weakness and strength, their power and glory, apostasies, their crimes, their righteousness and iniquity; . . . He was

According to the account, we all wept as a result, revealing our own lack of capacity as well as our doubt that anyone would willingly accept such a plan. Perhaps we felt all was lost.

And then, almost out of nowhere, someone stepped forward.

The person who first stepped forward is described in the scriptures as "like unto God" (Abraham 3:24), the "Only Begotten" (Doctrine and Covenants 76:25), and "Beloved and Chosen from the beginning" (Moses 4:2) who was "in the bosom of the Father" (John 1:18). His name was Jehovah, "the Great I AM" (Doctrine and Covenants 38:1). He possessed the requisite worthiness such that His assumption of sin and death would provide sufficient mercy to appease the demands of justice (see Alma 42:13) so that the Father's plan could be initiated as outlined. His character underwrote the plan to ensure it would be fulfilled. To the Father, and in earshot of each of us, He said, "Here am I, send me. . . . Thy will be done, and the glory be thine forever" (Moses 4:1–2). Even though the plan's beginning would be dependent upon His worthiness, He understood that the plan would ensure our ability for continued growth because all of the covenantal promises would be fulfilled, and all of the glory would be ascribed to the Father.

However, the Father's plan was not without risk. He knew that by securing individual agency, He was making it possible for some of His sons and daughters to be lost. This is because "it requires two parties to make a covenant, and those parties must be agreed, or no covenant can be made."[34] So what Jehovah acknowledged to all of us in the Council was that accepting His works to initiate the plan would perpetuate the Father's covenant with them. But anyone who would reject His efforts would terminate the covenant and prevent further individual advancement. Both the Father and Jehovah knew this scenario was a natural outcome of preserving moral agency.

---

acquainted with the situation of all nations and with their destiny; he ordered all things according to the council of his own will. He knows the situation of both the living and the dead; and has made ample provision for their redemption, according to their several circumstances, and the laws of the kingdom of God, whether in this world, or in the world to come." *The Joseph Smith Papers, Documents, Volume 9: December 1841–April 1842*, 377.

34. *The Joseph Smith Papers, Documents, Volume 2: July 1831–January 1833*, 351.

CHAPTER 4: JESUS CHRIST AND THE PLAN OF THE GREAT GOD

This fact provided an opening for the second individual to provide an alternative path for initiating the plan but with modifications that carried eternal implications for each of us. As the Prophet Joseph described the situation, the alternative plan created a division within the Grand Council. He explained, "The contention in heaven was [that Jehovah] said there would be certain souls that would not be saved; and [Lucifer] said he could save them all, and laid his plans before the grand council, who gave their vote in favor of [Jehovah]. So, [Lucifer] rose up in rebellion against [the Most High] God, and was cast down, with all who put up their heads for him."[35]

Lucifer, the second to step forward (Isaiah 14:12–14), was a formidable soul. He is described as "an angel who was in authority in the presence of God" (Doctrine and Covenants 76:25) and a "Son of the morning" (Isaiah 14:12)—two phrases that suggest he was one of the first spirit children of our Heavenly Father.[36]

Lacking the requisite "worthiness" of Jehovah, Lucifer suggested modifications to the plan that would benefit him personally by terminating our existing covenant with our Father and transferring us into an agreement with him:

Behold, here am I, send me, I will be thy son, and I will redeem all mankind, that one soul shall not be lost, and surely I will do it; wherefore give me thine honor. . . .

Wherefore, because that Satan rebelled against me, and sought to destroy the agency of man, which I, the Lord God, had given him, and also, that I should give unto him mine own power [or honor]; by the power of mine Only Begotten, I caused that he should be cast down. (Moses 4:1, 3)

Instead of the plan hinging upon the worthiness of "the Father's Only Begotten Son," an aspect that would require all of us to exercise our moral agency through faith, obedience, and sacrifice to obtain the promises of the covenant, Lucifer sought to usurp the position of the "Only Begotten" and rebel against the Father's covenant—a covenant that had brought each of us, including himself, to that point of

---

35. Discourse, 7 April 1844, as Published in *Times and Seasons*, 616, josephsmith-papers.org.

36. See Bruce R. McConkie, *Mormon Doctrine*, 2nd ed. (1966), 744.

47

spiritual progression. In short, he sought to elevate himself above our Father, "the Most High God" (see Isaiah 14:12–14).

Lucifer's required price for redeeming all mankind required the Father to give him His "honor" (Moses 4:1). The Father's honor and "glory is to bring to pass the immortality and eternal life of man" (Moses 1:39), which He accomplishes, as we have seen, by extending a new and everlasting covenant to others. Therefore, the price of Lucifer's proposal carried real implications for all of our eternal development, including our Father's. Our Father would have to terminate His covenant relationship with us, an act that would have violated His character as an "unchangeable Being" (Mormon 9:19) and His own word as a merciful and just God. If He had done so, He would have ceased to be God (see Alma 42:13).

Lucifer's selfish plan—notice the self-promotion through the use of the pronoun "I"—would have destroyed our agency. What the Most High acknowledged and nurtured from the first "starting point" was our autonomy as individual intelligences with the potential to progress through the exercise of our moral agency. Lucifer's proposal would ensure salvation for all, which on its face sounds very inclusive, loving, and appealing. However, it would have terminated God's new and everlasting covenant with us. Once ended, our eternal progression would have ceased because we would have surrendered our autonomy for a false security of salvation—a salvation decoupled from promises as heirs in exchange for eternal servitude to Lucifer, becoming "angels to the devil" (Jacob 3:11), subjected to his will and his power forever.

Fortunately for all of us, both our Father and the majority of the Council chose the worthiness of Jehovah, as He was allowed to take the book from the Father, initiate the plan (see Revelation 5:5–7), and assume the role as Mediator of the covenant (Hebrews 12:24). Job records that we all "shouted together and sang for joy" when we learned the news (Job 38:7).

Mediator of the New Covenant

A mediator is a person who helps negotiate two parties who are at odds with each other. On its face, that may seem strange given our covenant relationship with God. However, according to God's foreknowledge of all things, He foresaw that we would quickly and

CHAPTER 4: JESUS CHRIST AND THE PLAN OF THE GREAT GOD

knowingly violate eternal laws and become unclean during our second estate in mortality, thus separating ourselves from His presence, which no unclean thing can enter. So it became essential that God provide a way to reclaim and restore us, but it required the help of another. As discussed, Jehovah was both willing and able to act as the plan's Mediator, pay our collective debt to eternal justice, and restore us again to His presence after our mortal experience and testing. Amulek explained:

> For it is expedient that an atonement should be made; for according to the great plan of the Eternal God there must be an atonement made, or else all mankind must unavoidably perish; yea, all are hardened; yea, all are fallen and are lost, and must perish except it be through the atonement which it is expedient should be made.
>
> For it is expedient that there should be a great and last sacrifice; yea, not a sacrifice of man, neither of beast, neither of any manner of fowl; for it shall not be a human sacrifice; but it must be an infinite and eternal sacrifice. . . .
>
> And behold, this is the whole meaning of the law, every whit pointing to that great and last sacrifice; and that great and last sacrifice will be the Son of God, yea, infinite and eternal.
>
> And thus he shall bring salvation to all those who shall believe on his name; this being the intent of this last sacrifice, to bring about the bowels of mercy, which overpowereth justice, and bringeth about means unto men that they may have faith unto repentance.
>
> And thus mercy can satisfy the demands of justice, and encircles them in the arms of safety, while he that exercises no faith unto repentance is exposed to the whole law of the demands of justice; therefore only unto him that has faith unto repentance is brought about the great and eternal plan of redemption. (Alma 34:9–10, 14–16)

Without the intercession of a Mediator, the plan of salvation would fall apart, for there is no salvation, no hope, and no good thing without Him. The Father's covenant to all of His children—even the new and everlasting covenant—is but idle words without the Christ, who underwrites the promise of the Father to each of us. Because of the Great Mediator, we have a path forward: "[We] are free to choose liberty and eternal life, through the great Mediator of all men" (2 Nephi 2:27).

The War in Heaven

The Father's investment into the eternal growth of each of us was such that He cast Lucifer out of His presence. Consequently, Lucifer became Perdition,[37] "a son of the morning," and we all wept[38] because of him (Doctrine and Covenants 76:26–27). However, neither Lucifer nor those who preferred his proposal went quietly, and a conflict ensued between Lucifer and his followers and Jehovah and His. The scriptures describe the conflict as a "war in heaven" (Joseph Smith Translation, Revelation 12:6–8), a phrase suggesting that the disagreements were not just philosophical over who had the best methods. No, Lucifer proposed a violent takeover for control of the spiritual capital covenanted to the Father. He wanted us at any cost.

To Lucifer, our allegiance should be rewarded by positional authority over who acts as "the son of God" (Moses 4:1), not through principles of righteousness, such as gentleness, meekness, persuasion, kindness, or love unfeigned (Doctrine and Covenants 121:41). The battle commenced because of Lucifer's competitive desire to ascend over everyone and everything (see Isaiah 14:13–14). Lucifer demonstrated—after receiving just a little authority—the sad tendency for beings to exercise unrighteous dominion (Doctrine and Covenants 121:34–40). He was tempted and succumbed—like most men and women do—to the gratification of his pride, vain ambition, and tendency to exercise control and compulsion by means of his positional authority.

---

37. The word *perdition* began as a word meaning "utter destruction." The word was borrowed into English in the fourteenth century from Anglo-French *perdiciun* and ultimately derives from the Latin verb *perdere*, meaning "to destroy." *Perdere* was formed by combining the prefix *per-* ("through") and *dare* ("to give"). *Merriam-Webster.com Dictionary*, s.v. "perdition," accessed August 6, 2024, https://www.merriam-webster.com/dictionary/perdition.

38. Did we all weep because of the feeling of loss, losing one of our own who we knew well and loved? Perhaps. This phrase could also imply that we wept as a result of him, meaning that his efforts after being cast down caused us to weep and mourn.

CHAPTER 4: JESUS CHRIST AND THE PLAN OF THE GREAT GOD

Lucifer was cunning in his efforts, which is why "a third part of the hosts of heaven" were turned away (Revelation 12:4; Doctrine and Covenants 29:35). The phrase "third part" may be significant to understand the effect of Lucifer's message in the Grand Council. Many interpret the phrase as one-third of all of the spirit children of our heavenly parents; however, if the Grand Council consisted of many parts, and those parts were not evenly distributed with spirits, then "a third part" would be a different number of spirits—perhaps far fewer spirits—who were persuaded by Lucifer and who turned away.

Whatever the size of his premortal following, Lucifer rose up against Jehovah and His number one agent, Michael,[39] who the scriptures speak of as "the archangel," which in Hebrew means "who is like God." Michael led the conflict with faith in the "worthiness" of Jehovah, which provided Him (and all of the spirit children who followed the Father's plan) power to cast Lucifer and his followers out of heaven and into the still-to-be-created Earth (Revelation 12:9). This battle served as a sign of what would be continued on earth (see Joseph Smith Translation, Revelation 12:1, 4). What Lucifer sought and what was denied him in the Grand Council—namely, "the kingdom of our God and his Christ" (Doctrine and Covenants 76:28)—he continues to pursue on earth by luring away as many of God's spirit children away from the covenant as he can: "Wherefore, he maketh war with the saints of God, and encompasseth them round about" (Doctrine and Covenants 76:29).

---

39. Michael is identified in latter-day revelation as Adam (see Doctrine and Covenants 27:11) and has been engaged from the beginning in building and defending the kingdom of God in heaven, on earth, and in the final scenes of this earth (see Revelation 12:7; Daniel 10:13, 21; 12:1; Doctrine and Covenants 29:26; 88:112–115). He was first given authority in the Grand Council to act on behalf of Jehovah in all things (see Doctrine and Covenants 78:16). Joseph Smith explained, ""The Priesthood was first given to Adam; he obtained the First Presidency, and held the keys of it from generation to generation. He obtained it in the Creation, before the world was formed. . . . When [priesthood keys] are revealed from heaven, it is by Adam's authority." *The Joseph Smith Papers, Documents, Volume 6: June 26–August 4, 1839*, 542. Given this information, we understand more clearly why Satan so thoroughly dismisses and attacks Adam—his origins, reality, and motives—through various methods.

UNPARDONABLE SIN

What became of those spirit sons and daughters who chose Lucifer's proposal over the new and everlasting covenant? They were cast down to Earth with Satan, or Perdition, and became his sons and daughters, or sons of Perdition.[40] Like Lucifer, they received no physical body and remain as spirits with no path for further growth or development. In a word, they have been damned. Why? It is because they rejected the new and everlasting covenant and, as a result, committed a sin that is unpardonable, or the unpardonable sin. What is the unpardonable sin? Joseph Smith explained it this way:

> What must a man do to commit the unpardonable sin? He must receive the Holy Ghost, have the heavens opened unto him, and know God, and then sin against Him. After a man has sinned against the Holy Ghost, there is no repentance for him. He has got to say that the sun does not shine while he sees it; he has got to deny Jesus Christ when the heavens have been opened unto him, and to deny the plan of salvation with his eyes open to the truth of it.[41]

Joseph indicates a few conditions in order to commit the unpardonable sin. First, a person must receive the Holy Ghost through the ordained channel, which is the laying on of hands by one who holds the Melchizedek Priesthood. Second, they must possess a witness from the Holy Ghost of the plan of salvation, or, more specifically, the new and everlasting covenant.

I used to believe that it was the witness of the Holy Ghost of God's reality that brought condemnation, but that is only partially true. The full explanation includes knowledge of the new and everlasting

---

40. We assume that the term "sons of Perdition" includes both men and women and that the term *sons* is applied generally as "man" or "mankind" is applied to the human race as a whole (see Bruce R. McConkie, *Mormon Doctrine*, 746, where he associates the term *sons* with *followers*). However, it is possible that those who followed Lucifer were only males and that the term *sons* is used specifically for the affected audience, just as "sons of Helaman" is used in reference to the two thousand young men who followed Helaman into battle.

41. Joseph Smith, "The King Follett Discourse," 10, accessed August 6, 2024, https://emp.byui.edu/jexj/new/talks/talks/JS%20KingFollettDiscourse.pdf.

Chapter 4: Jesus Christ and the Plan of the Great God

covenant, which is the authorized channel through which the Holy Ghost administers. President Joseph Fielding Smith explained:

> Through the Holy Ghost the truth is woven into the very fibre and sinews of the body so that it cannot be forgotten. So positive and powerful are the teachings of the Spirit that when a man [or woman] receives this knowledge and partakes of this power of God, which can only come after receiving the covenants and obligations belonging to the new and everlasting covenant, and he then turns away from this knowledge and these covenants, he sins knowingly.[42]

Those premortal spirit brothers and sisters of ours committed the unpardonable sin[43] because they knew the covenant of the Father to each of them, had the plan presented to them—including the Savior's role as the Mediator of the covenant—and then turned away, thus "denying the powers of God" (powers they had received through the Father's covenant from their "starting point") and "denying the Only Begotten Son," bringing both the Father and the Son "into open shame" (see Hebrews 6:4–6; Doctrine and Covenants 76:34–35). The penalty for these souls is to suffer the second death, a penalty that the new and everlasting covenant explicitly guards against.[44] The consequence of such choices has always carried severe consequences.

Knowledge of the new and everlasting covenant brings great promises, but for those who have received it, it carries ultimate accountability toward God. Imagine hearing these words in the Grand Council from our Father as He presented His plan to us:

---

42. Joseph Fielding Smith, *Doctrines of Salvation*, comp. Bruce R. McConkie (1955), 1:48.

43. Mercifully, there are limited opportunities in which this sin can be committed. It appears the first instance was in the Grand Council and the only instance since then when the sin can be committed is during our mortal life in our second estate (i.e., not in the spirit world, which is also in our second estate). Joseph Smith taught, "No man can commit the unpardonable sin after the dissolution of the body, nor in this life, until he receives the Holy Ghost, but they must do it in this world." "King Follett Discourse," 10.

44. See the section "Not Being Hurt by the Second Death" in chapter 3 of this book.

Therefore, prepare thy heart to receive and obey the instructions which I am about to give unto you; for all those who have this law revealed unto them must obey the same.

For behold, I reveal unto you a new and an everlasting covenant; and if ye abide not that covenant, then are ye damned; for no one can reject this covenant and be permitted to enter into my glory.

For all who will have a blessing at my hands shall abide the law which was appointed for that blessing, and the conditions thereof, as were instituted from before the foundation of the world.

And as pertaining to the new and everlasting covenant, it was instituted for the fulness of my glory; and he that receiveth a fulness thereof must and shall abide the law, or he shall be damned, saith the Lord God. (Doctrine and Covenants 132:3–6)

What we learned in the Grand Council was that a path existed for tremendous promise and eternal expansion. At the same time, we learned this was the only way forward. The new and everlasting covenant was the law instituted by our Father for the fulness of His glory, and we chose to accept it.

Testing Within the Covenant

Now that the plan was secured or ensured by the worthiness of Jehovah, additional steps were taken to enable the plan. The Lord revealed to Joseph Smith that "an everlasting covenant was made between three personages before the organization of this earth and relates to their dispensation of things to men on the earth. These personages . . . are called God the first, the Creator; God the second, the Redeemer; and God the third, the Witness or Testator."

The agreement between these three personages established a ruling body, known as "One Eternal God," with a shared responsibility to oversee individual progress against covenant requirements and apply the laws of eternal justice and the plan of mercy—known as Final Judgment (see Alma 44:11).

Final Judgment is the time when the laws of eternal justice are exercised and the punishment affixed to the laws is executed (see Alma 42:13–16). It is when the effects of our deeds done in the body will be evaluated (see Doctrine and Covenants 1:10)—when our thoughts,

CHAPTER 4: JESUS CHRIST AND THE PLAN OF THE GREAT GOD

words, and works (see Alma 12:14) will be made plain before us "with perfect recollection" (Alma 11:43). Reflecting on this reality more often than we now do would help us live a little better than we now live.

Final Judgment is also the time when the Mediator of the covenant advocates for us to bring to pass the plan of our Father's mercy (see Doctrine and Covenants 45:3–5). Our Father did not send us to earth to fail but to learn more perfectly about what we really want—learning that comes as we are subjected to enticements toward our minds, bodies, and spirits. Final Judgment is a highly personalized and perfectly equitable affair, as applied by the Godhead on our behalf. As such, it serves as our primary motivation for regulating our behavior on earth to live within the light given to us to guide our thoughts and actions. Therefore, we had perfect confidence in the Grand Council that we would be judged with wisdom and order. Concerning the beauty of our Father's judgment, Joseph Smith explained:

> The Great Parent of the universe looks upon the whole human family with a fatherly care and paternal regard. He views them as His offspring; and without any of those contracted feelings that influence the children of men. . . . He holds the reins of judgment in his hands. He is a wise lawgiver, and will judge all men, not according to the narrow, contracted notions of men, but according to the deeds done in the body whether they be good or evil. . . . He will judge them not according to what they have not, but according to what they have, "those who have lived without law, will be judged without law," and those who have a law will be judged by that law. We need not doubt the wisdom and intelligence of the Great Jehovah, He will award judgment or mercy to all nations according to their several deserts, their means of obtaining intelligence, the laws by which they are governed, the facilities afforded them of obtaining correct information, and his inscrutable designs in relation to the human family. And when the designs of God shall be made manifest, and the curtain of futurity be withdrawn, we shall all of us eventually have to confess that the judge of all the earth has done right.[45]

---

45. Joseph Smith, in *History of the Church*, 4:595–96; from "Baptism for the Dead," an editorial published in *Times and Seasons*, Apr. 15, 1842, 759.

We knew that the judgment—our Final Judgment—would trigger our resurrection and determine the glory we would inherit, according to the covenant, and we had full confidence that on that future day, "all of us eventually have to confess that the judge of all the earth has done right."

To each of us, the plan promised birth on the soon-to-be-created Earth, where we would receive a physical body and begin learning in a laboratory environment. On Earth, we would become subjects to follow after our own wills (see Alma 42:7). Additionally, we could be tested through trials of faith, obedience, and sacrifice in the covenant and experience death as a portal to the covenantal promise of a resurrection—or restoration—to an immortal body like our heavenly parents. All that was needed now was a place to start, where the dimension of time could be applied on our behalf, where a veil could be activated to protect us from what we knew of the covenant and our Father's glory (see Doctrine and Covenants 101:23) so our testing could begin. What we needed was the creation of an earth.

Chapter Summary

1. Our Father presented to us a plan of salvation to further our pursuit of the promises of the new and everlasting covenant at a premortal Grand Council.

    a. The plan of salvation outlined the creation of the earth.
    b. The plan of salvation outlined our birth and the reception of a physical body.
    c. The plan of salvation outlined an additional period of testing.

2. The plan of salvation contains a plan of redemption upon which the entire plan hinges.

    a. The worthiness of Jehovah—premortal Jesus Christ— enabled Him to initiate the Father's plan of salvation, which He willingly offered to do.
    b. Lucifer—premortal Satan—offered an alternative to the Father's plan of salvation that would have dissolved

the new and everlasting covenant and our Father-child relationship with God.

   c. The different options prompted the War in Heaven where Jehovah and His followers fought against Lucifer and his followers. Jehovah prevailed and became our Mediator; Lucifer lost and was cast down with his followers.

   d. The unpardonable sin is a repudiation of the new and everlasting covenant and the Father-child relationship.

3. The new and everlasting covenant brings increased accountability toward God.

   a. The Godhead was organized in the Grand Council to oversee the testing of us in the new and everlasting covenant in mortality.

   b. Final Judgment is set for each person to account for their testing in the new and everlasting covenant.

   c. Our Heavenly Father ensures that all will be fairly evaluated during the Final Judgment.

   d. Jesus is our Advocate during the Final Judgment.

REFLECTION QUESTIONS

- What aspects of the new and everlasting covenant stood out to you in this chapter?
- What are some connections between the promises of the new and everlasting covenant and our need to be tested in mortality?
- What differences did you notice between our Father's plan of salvation and Lucifer's alternative?
- Why was Jehovah uniquely qualified to fulfill the plan of redemption?
- How do the Godhead's different roles influence and bless your life on Earth?
- Who do you know who would benefit from what you have learned?

5

THREE PILLARS OF ETERNITY

IN PHYSICAL TERMS, A PILLAR IS A COLUMN—USUALLY MADE OF STONE or steel—that provides support for a building or structure. Metaphorically speaking, a pillar is a dimension that fills a plan with assurance of fulfillment. In reference to our Father's plan of salvation, three pillars provide such confidence that the plan will be realized and the promises of the covenant assured. They are the creation of the earth, the Fall of Adam and Eve, and the Atonement of Jesus Christ.[46] These critical events underscore eternity, even our path to eternal lives, as promised by the new and everlasting covenant.

THE CREATION OF THE EARTH

The Creation was one of the first ways our Father began manifesting the promises of the covenant to us. Through the creation of the earth, we receive a place to inhabit and are given an opportunity to advance. We receive "an earth, whereupon we may dwell to see if we will do all things whatsoever the Lord shall command [us]" (Abraham 3:25). Knowing as we then did that "the meek of the earth shall inherit [it]" (Matthew 5:5), this earth provides us with the promise of an everlasting inheritance, provided we fulfill our obligations of the

---

46. See Bruce R. McConkie, "Christ and the Creation," *Ensign*, June 1982, 9–15.

covenant. We are obligated to care for the earth, for our bodies, and for one another, acting as our brother's keeper.

The earth and its necessary cosmic ecosystem were first formed spiritually before it was made physically (see Doctrine and Covenants 29:31–32; Moses 3:5; Abraham 5:3). This implies a planning phase of the Creation, similar to an architect creating a blueprint before builders put shovels in the ground. It also implies the Father's use of His faith in His covenant to influence creation to organize first spiritually and then temporally. In other words, just as in the case with the formation of our spiritual bodies, everything the Father creates has a spirit, with a will to act for itself and obey.

Additionally, the physical creation of earth did not come from nothing—it was not the result, that is, of "creatio ex nihilo." Instead, it came from elements that have always existed (see Doctrine and Covenants 93:33). In Hebrew, to *create* implies to "organize, the same as a man would organize the materials to build a ship."[47] Thus, our Father brought materials together that already existed to create this world. How did He organize them? By what power? Through the same power and method He used to bring our spirits into existence: by priesthood power exercised "by persuasion, by long-suffering, by gentleness and meekness, and by love unfeigned" (Doctrine and Covenants 121:41).[48] This means that God used His words to persuade the materials to organize according to His will. It took our Father's faith in the covenant manifested through His words to fully organize the earth.[49]

Our earth, and everything in it, has been placed in a position to act for itself (see Doctrine and Covenants 88:36–39).[50] The creative

---

47. Joseph Smith, "The King Follett Discourse," 7, accessed August 6, 2024, https://emp.byui.edu/jexj/new/talks/talks/JS%20KingFollettDiscourse.pdf.

48. "Priesthood . . . is the law by which the worlds are, were, and will continue for ever and ever." *Discourses of Brigham Young*, sel. John A. Widtsoe (Salt Lake City, UT: Deseret Book, 1941), 130.

49. God worked by "mental exertion instead of physical force. It is by words instead of exerting his physical powers with which every being works when he works by faith." *Lectures on Faith* (1985), 72.

50. In these verses, the term *kingdom* is also used to describe "beings," which I understand applies to all elements within the universe, to both act and to be

element's freedom to act was demonstrated during the creative process. The role of the Creator was to work through words and "[watch] those things which they had ordered until they obeyed" (Abraham 4:18). Hugh Nibley explained the process this way: "The Gods worked through agents. . . . What they ordered was not the completed product, but the process to bring it about, providing a scheme under which life might expand; 'Let us prepare the earth to bring forth grass,' not 'Let us create grass.'"[51]

The creation of the earth was also not completed by our Father alone but was a collective activity led by Jehovah—"the Great I AM . . . the same which looked upon the wide expanse of eternity, and all the seraphic hosts of heaven, before the world was made" (Doctrine and Covenants 6:1)—and Michael, with tasks delegated to others.[52]

The book of Abraham uses the term *we* to describe the creative enterprise: "We will go down, for there is space there, and we will take of these materials, and we will make an earth whereon these may dwell" (Abraham 3:25). Again, Nibley explains it this way: "The principle of maximum participation, of the active cooperation of all of God's creatures in the working out of his plans, which, in fact, are devised for their benefit . . . [means that] everybody gets into the act. Every creature, to the limit of its competence, is given the supreme compliment of being left on its own, so that the word 'obey' is correctly applied."[53]

President Joseph Smith, in his grand vision of the redemption of the dead, identified the "noble and great ones" who participated in the creative process as mentioned by Abraham and "received their first lessons in the world of spirits" (Doctrine and Covenants 138:56). Perhaps it was not just prophets who were among the noble and great ones, but all those called to lead within the Lord's kingdom on earth participated in the creative enterprise in premortality. The creation

---

acted upon. For example, even at the atomic level, protons and electrons (kingdoms/beings) have laws that govern their relationship to each other and where they exercise their agency to obey relative to those laws.

51. Hugh Nibley, *Old Testament and Related Studies* (Salt Lake City, UT: Deseret Book, 1986), 70.

52. See *The Joseph Smith Papers, Documents, Volume 6: June 26–August 4, 1839*, 542.

53. Hugh Nibley, *Old Testament and Related Studies*, 71.

of the earth involved those who embraced the new and everlasting covenant in the process of building the mansion they were promised to inherit.

Our Physical Earth

Our earth is a creative miracle. It was created not only as the ideal place for us to learn and develop, but it also has all the necessary protections to ensure our safety. Beyond what is described in the scriptural account, the earth was designed within a broader ecosystem, with vital characteristics that sustain and nurture life and enable us—the earth's intended inhabitants—to fill the measure of our creation. The characteristics of this complex and dynamic ecosystem are a wonder and include such things as:

1. A perfect position within the solar system (Goldilocks Zone): Earth is in a not-too-hot and not-too-cold zone that ensures water won't boil away (as with Venus) or freeze (as with Mars).
2. Ozone layer: The Earth's ozone layer protects us from harmful UV rays (radiation) from our sun.
3. Magnetic field: Generated from molten lava in the Earth's core, the magnetic field acts as a repellent shield against solar winds that would strip away our atmosphere.
4. Proximity to gas giants: The gravity of Jupiter and Saturn protect the Earth from meteorites and other interstellar objects
5. Relatively large moon: Our moon ensures that the Earth's axial tilt limits extreme atmospheric events and provides for ecological evolution and the perpetuation of complex life forms.
6. Active plate tectonics: Unique in our solar system, the Earth recycles carbon through volcanic events, which provides diverse habitats and a stable climate (in geological terms).
7. Ideal atmospheric composition: The Earth's atmosphere is composed primarily of nitrogen, oxygen, and carbon dioxide that allows for respiration, supports various life forms, and maintains the planet's temperature while also protecting against solar radiation and space projectiles like meteorites.
8. An abundance of water: 71% of the Earth's surface is covered

in water, which is a solvent for life and provides necessary chemical reactions for diverse species to thrive, helps regulate planetary temperature, and provides habitats for many organisms.

9. Perfect size and mass: The Earth's size-mass ratio is perfect for holding on to its atmosphere and water and securing tectonic plate motion to replenish its resources. The Earth's size-mass ratio also provides the ideal amount of gravity to make living enjoyable.

10. Stable and reliable sun: Our sun provides the right amount of warmth and light over billions of years to allow creation to grow, thrive, evolve, and diversify.[54]

Clearly, the Father was mindful of each of His spirit sons and daughters in the design of this planetary system, thoughtfully accounting for all of our development needs while lovingly providing us with an opportunity to participate in its miraculous formation. In a future millennial day, we will learn more about this miraculous creative process, our involvement in it, and the fulness of its purpose in our covenant promises (Doctrine and Covenants 101:32–33). With the creation of the world accomplished, the stage was set for populating it—and that required the introduction of our first parents, Adam and Eve.

The Fall of Adam and Eve

The capstone of the creation of the earth was the creation of physical bodies for Adam and Eve. With them came the hope of us all. Into each of them, and eventually into each of us, the Father "breathed into their nostrils the breath of life and [they] became living souls" (see Genesis 2:7; Moses 3:7; Abraham 5:7). In Hebrew, the covenant name for Jehovah is spelled YHWH and pronounced Yah-Way. When God put into our first parents the breath of life, He encoded into their very breath the acknowledgment of His existence and covenant with them. As we inhale, we begin the name of God (Yah) and with every

---

54. Ideas summarized from Weird World, "Ten 'lucky coincidences' that combine together to make Earth a suitable home for life," Facebook, June 30, 2023, https://fb.watch/tONNkKJrl8/?mibextid=2Rb1fB.

exhale (Way), we complete the name of God,[55] remembering that our lives are a gift with covenant obligation. Such was provided to Adam and Eve from the beginning and to each of us at the time of our beginning on earth.

Both Adam and Eve were created in the image of our heavenly parents and given dominion over the earth to tend to it, take care of it, and enjoy it (see Moses 2:26–30; Genesis 1:26–27; Abraham 4:24–31). To have dominion meant that the earth fell under priesthood keys that Adam had received from the Lord.[56] This dominion would follow Adam and Eve forward through the process of the Fall, from a paradisiacal or terrestrial state to a telestial state of existence. Paul explained that the earth fell, or "was made subject to vanity, not willingly, but by reason of him who has subjected the same in hope" (Romans 8:20), meaning that the earth, which was perfectly obedient during the Creation, did not naturally want to fall but did so because it honored Adam and Eve's choice to fall. Like us, Mother Earth and all of creation knew that the path forward required a temporal experience, and so it exercised faith in the "earnest expectation" provided to it from the Father and "waiteth for the manifestation of the sons of God . . . because the creature itself also shall be delivered from the bondage of corruption into the glorious liberty of the children of God" (Romans 8:19–22).

Adam was known premortally as Michael, the same "who is like God" and fought alongside Jehovah in the War in Heaven. To him, the Lord conferred the Melchizedek Priesthood[57] along with the necessary priesthood keys to introduce mortality to all the spirit chil-

---

55. See Rabbi Shlomo Schachter, "The Breath of Life," Ohr Torah Stone, Sept. 5, 2021, https://ots.org.il/the-breath-of-life/. In Hebrew, the verb often translated as *soul* in the King James Bible is closely associated with the words "breath," "Spirit," and "exhale."

56. See *The Joseph Smith Papers, Documents, Volume 6: June 26–August 4, 1839*, 542.

57. "The Priesthood was first given to Adam; he obtained the First Presidency and held the keys of it from generation to generation. He obtained it in the Creation, before the world was formed. . . . He was called of God to this office and was the father of all living in this day, and to him was given dominion. These men held keys first on earth, and then in heaven." *The Joseph Smith Papers, Volume 6*, 542.

dren of God and to oversee all methods of revelation from God to man.[58] He was created "to open the way of the world and to dress the garden."[59] Our view of him premortally and his role in the salvation of this earth is dramatically expanded from modern-day revelations through the Prophet Joseph Smith.

His name has a variety of meanings within the scriptures, sometimes referring to a particular man, the first husband, mankind, or as a proper name or title.[60] The earliest texts of our Old Testament most often use *Adam* as a person but rarely—only once—as a personal name. Additionally, Adam "plays a surprising number of roles, each with a different persona, a different name, a different environment, a different office, and calling,"[61] which means we should acknowledge that Adam is meant to change. He is not a static figure sent to earth to live and die; instead, he is intended to become something more than what he was when he arrived on the scene. As such, Adam—using the name in the collective male/female/mankind sense—is our model. Each of us is to follow his lead, change, evolve, learn, and grow over the course of our lives. In other words, each of us is to consider ourselves as if we are Adam.

Eve brought with her the potential of "many" lives (Moses 4:26). Her body—and the bodies of billions and billions of women who would come after her—would provide the sacred space to recreate what the Father provided to Adam and Eve together, even living souls where the spirit could be meshed together with a physical body and create the physical, individual condition where one could receive a fulness of joy (see Doctrine and Covenants 93:33)—or, in other

---

58. "The [priesthood] keys have to be brought from heaven whenever the gospel is sent. When they are revealed from heaven, it is by Adam's authority. . . . He is the father of the human family, and presides over the spirits of all men, and all that have had the keys must stand before him in this grand council. . . . The Son of Man stands before him, and there is given him glory and dominion. Adam delivers up his stewardship to Christ, that which was delivered to him as holding the keys of the universe but retains his standing as head of the human family." *The Joseph Smith Papers, Volume 6*, 542.

59. *Teachings of the Prophet Joseph Smith*, sel. Joseph Fielding Smith (1938), 12.

60. Cited in Hugh Nibley, *Old Testament and Related Studies*, 78–79.

61. Hugh Nibley, *Old Testament and Related Studies*, 77.

words, realize the promises of the covenant. In short, Eve was created to "be the mother of all living" (Moses 4:26).[62] Thus, from before the Creation, Eve was endowed with a deep desire to fulfill the plan through the bearing of children, as President Nelson explained: "Eve came as a partner, to build and to organize the bodies of mortal men. She was designed by Deity to co-create and nurture life, that the great plan of the Father might achieve fruition. Eve 'was the mother of all living' (Moses 4:26). She was the first of all women."[63]

It was Eve who first recognized the path forward by partaking of the forbidden fruit, meaning the conditions to make oneself mortal and thereby capable of bearing children. The Prophet Joseph Smith indicated that the Lord breathed into her not a single life—as He had done with Adam—but "the breath of lives,"[64] indicative of this special endowment of discernment and reproductive capacity.

Adam and Eve were first married by the Lord before they were introduced into the Garden of Eden (see Genesis 2:24–25; Moses 3:25; Abraham 5:18–19). Hence, their commitment to each other as help meets and equal partners was established before their Fall. Together they modeled the covenant path for the earth "to fill the measure of its creation" (Doctrine and Covenants 49:16), according to the covenant. At the time of their creation, Adam and Eve were clothed with light,[65] indicating that their station was one of a different order—a paradisiacal order (see Articles of Faith 1:10). "The first temporal creation of all things was paradisiacal in nature" explained Elder Bruce R. McConkie, "In the primeval and Edenic day all forms of life lived in a higher and different state than now prevails. The coming fall would take them downward and forward and onward. Death and

---

62. In this way, Eve was a model of Jesus Christ, our Redeemer, who uses His body vicariously to mesh our spirits and bodies together eternally through a glorious resurrection. Physical birth is modeled after our spiritual birth through Jesus Christ.

63. Russell M. Nelson, "Lessons from Eve," *Ensign*, Nov. 1987, 87.

64. History, 1838–1856, volume D-1 [1 August 1842–1 July 1843], 1552, josephsmithpapers.org.

65. "The Words of the Luminaries" in the Dead Sea Scrolls (4Q504) alludes to Adam's pre-existent glory in the Garden of Eden before his Fall.

procreation had yet to enter the world. That death would be Adam's gift to man."[66]

Prior to partaking of the forbidden fruit, Adam and Eve had forgotten what they knew before the Creation, and they were innocent before God (see Doctrine and Covenants 93:38). They were limited to what the Father had taught them since introducing them to the Garden of Eden. Yet "the Fall was made possible because an infinite Creator . . . made the earth and man and all forms of life in such a state that they could fall. This fall involved a change of status. All things were so created that they could fall or change, and thus was introduced the type and kind of existence needed to put into operation all of the terms and conditions of the Father's eternal plan of salvation."[67] This means that Adam and Eve brought with them their unique spiritual gifts to further the plan of salvation, in spite of their "state of innocence, having no joy, for they knew no misery; doing no good, for they knew no sin" (2 Nephi 2:23).

Endowed with their agency to act, Adam and Eve needed the conditions to exercise their agency. They could not be compelled to act by God or by anyone else, for that would destroy the very plan that guaranteed their freedom to choose. However, they could be "enticed" (2 Nephi 2:16) to choose if an opposition to God's commandments could be provided. Both Adam and Eve had been "instructed sufficiently that they knew good from evil" (2 Nephi 2:5), and they had received the "Spirit of Christ . . . to know good from evil . . . to know with a perfect knowledge [what was] of God" (Moroni 7:16). Therefore, God provided an "opposition in all things . . . that righteousness might be brought to pass," that all things might not remain "a compound in one," where neither life nor death, corruption nor incorruption, happiness nor misery, sense nor sensibility could be brought to pass (2 Nephi 2:11). Wherefore, "after [God] had created our first parents . . . he created an opposition, even the forbidden fruit in opposition to the tree of life; the one being sweet and the other bitter" (2 Nephi 2:15).

---

66. Bruce R. McConkie, "Christ and the Creation," 9. In this way, Adam is a model of Jesus Christ, "for as in Adam all die, even so in Christ shall all be made alive" (1 Corinthians 15:21–22).

67. Bruce R. McConkie, "Christ and the Creation," 9.

The New and Everlasting Covenant

In the Garden of Eden, our Heavenly Father gave Adam and Eve two commandments that were in conflict with one another. First, He commanded Adam to stay with Eve, his wife (see Abraham 5:18–19), explaining "that it was not good for man to be alone . . . and he should cleave unto his wife and become one flesh" (Moses 3:18, 24). Staying with Eve was Adam's first priority. Second, God instructed Adam and Eve that of all the trees in the garden, "they should not eat of the tree of knowledge of good and evil" (Moses 3:17), the penalty being death. So there Adam and Eve stood, essentially stuck between two trees—on the one hand, the tree of life, and on the other, the tree of knowledge of good and evil. They were stuck because so long as both commandments were kept, as Lehi explains, they "would not have fallen, but [they] would have remained in the garden of Eden. And all things which were created must have remained in the same state in which they were after they were created; and they must have remained forever, and had no end. And they would have had no children; wherefore they would have remained in a state of innocence, having no joy, for they knew no misery; doing no good, for they knew no sin" (2 Nephi 2:22–23)

Understanding the purpose behind the conflicting commandments, Lehi uses Hebrew parallelism to illustrate the choice facing Adam and Eve. Parallelism is when a writer introduces two concepts followed by two explanations that maintain the same relationship to one another. Notice that the forbidden fruit is related to "sweet," and the tree of life is related to "bitter." On its face, this may seem strange to us. We do not often think of the tree of life as bitter, but it is. Eve first realized—followed by Adam—that the only path out of the garden toward family life and growth was through partaking of the bitter fruits of opposition: through death, despair, and the pains of mortality. They may not have known why that path was better, but they felt from the "breath of life" within them that the fruit of the tree of knowledge of good and evil "was good for food, . . . pleasant to the eyes, and a tree to be desired to make [them] wise" (Moses 4:12). So they partook of the fruit of the tree of knowledge, meaning that they partook of the conditions of mortality and lost the limited light they had in order to gain infinitely more.

CHAPTER 5: THREE PILLARS OF ETERNITY

A few lessons from Adam and Eve. First, like them, we seldom have complete information upon which to act on what is right to gain more knowledge. "For how to act I did not know, and unless I could get more wisdom than I then had, I would never know" (Joseph Smith—History 1:12), said the boy Joseph Smith. But each of us, like Joseph and our first parents, "are instructed sufficiently to know good from evil," and if we will rely on the word of the Lord we have received and follow the voice of the Spirit within us, we will be led to the correct path our Father has prepared for us (see Doctrine and Covenants 84:44–46).

Second, the covenant path is a bitter path, and it is also the path that brings meaning to the fruit of the tree of life—as we will soon see. It is the path designed to test us, to try us, so that we can prove to ourselves—perfectly—who we really are and what we really want. Eve saw this possibility and proclaimed, "Were it not for our transgression we never should have had seed, and never should have known good and evil, and the joy of our redemption, and the eternal life which God giveth unto all the obedient" (Moses 5:11); or as Lehi summarized, "Adam fell that men might be; and men are, that they might have joy" (2 Nephi 2:25).

When Adam and Eve partook of the forbidden fruit and became mortal, they violated a commandment of God and lost their light; they became naked before God, without a covering. Men and women without a covenant are naked. Almost immediately after Adam and Eve partook of the fruit, our Father visited them in the garden to restore them to the covenant and provide a covering for their nakedness, an act that should illustrate to us who our Father is and what He is all about. He brings His Only Begotten to us: "And the Messiah cometh in the fulness of time, that he may redeem the children of men from the fall."

THE ATONEMENT OF JESUS CHRIST

The Fall of Adam and Eve ushered Jehovah into His role as Mediator between God the Father and His spirit children. Though He acted with many of the spirit sons and daughters in an ante-mortal capacity as creators of the earth under the direction of our Father, it would not be until after the Fall of Adam and Eve that Jehovah would begin to mediate the Father on our behalf. In the garden, with the Mediator in place, the Father began working exclusively through Jehovah on Adam and Eve's behalf. For example, at the Father's command, it was Jehovah who clothed Adam and Eve to cover their nakedness, it was Jehovah who set protections to guard the way to the tree of life, and it was Jehovah who drove Adam and Eve from the garden into the fallen telestial (mortal) world. From this point on, the Father would become invisible to Adam and Eve and only reintroduced through the person of His Only Begotten Son.[68] Thus, Adam and Eve and their posterity would need to "look to the great Mediator, and hearken unto his great commandments; and be faithful unto his words, and choose eternal life" (2 Nephi 2:28) in order to realize the promises of the Father to return to His presence.

After Adam and Eve fell, our Father instructed Jehovah—ante-mortal Jesus Christ—to provide a covering for them to hide their nakedness (see Genesis 3:21). The covering Jehovah provided the couple was an actual garment that covered their physical nakedness, and most importantly, it was a covering to cloak their sins. The Hebrew word for cover is *kafar*, which is the root word for *atonement*, indicating "to cover, . . . to wipe out, . . . to forgive . . . to be expiated."[69] Thus, by indicating their desire to follow Jesus Christ, Adam and Eve were clothed with a skin or garment of light as a covering for their nakedness as a constant reminder of the future Atonement of Jesus Christ. They figuratively were covered in the flesh of Jesus (see Hebrews 10:20). The Book of Mormon indicates that one promise of the covenant to the righteous, as we discussed in chapter 3, is a robe of righteousness, representing the promise to return to light (see 2 Nephi 9:14). In the garden, according to the commandment of our Father, Jehovah provided a symbol of that future covenantal promise to Adam and Eve.

Before driving Adam and Eve from the Garden of Eden, our Father made known unto Adam and Eve the plan of redemption through His Only Begotten Son and put them under covenant to keep several commandments to start them back on their path to His

---

68. See "Gospel Classics: The Father and the Son," *Ensign*, Apr. 2002.

69. Hugh Nibley, "The Atonement of Jesus Christ, Part 1," *Ensign*, July 1990.

presence. The commandments included caring for and cultivating the earth, multiplying and replenishing the earth through the bearing and rearing of children and teaching them the commandments, worshipping the Lord through the offering of sacrifices of the firstlings of their flocks, and calling upon God's name in prayer. And though they were shut out of His physical presence, the Father promised them He would speak unto them through His voice and the voice of messengers at a future time (see Moses 5:1–6). "Therefore," explained Alma, "God gave unto them commandments, after having made known unto them the plan of redemption, that they should not do evil, the penalty thereof being a second death, which was an everlasting death as to things pertaining unto righteousness; for on such the plan of redemption could have no power, for the works of justice could not be destroyed, according to the supreme goodness of God" (Alma 12:32). In short, our Father placed Adam and Eve—and through them their posterity—under covenant to obey His commandments and to offer sacrifices in the name of His Son.

The Atonement of Jesus Christ overcame the effects of Adam and Eve's Fall that were immediately transmitted to all of creation, including their future posterity—in other words, us. The first effect was the introduction of death to God's creative works. Adam and Eve knew that if they partook of the tree of knowledge, they would partake of the conditions to make them and all things under their dominion mortal, meaning that everything moved from a terrestrial or paradisiacal state to a telestial condition. A telestial condition is subject to death; thus, Adam and Eve partook of a condition where they could pass through the portal of physical death. This was according to God's instruction to them in the garden that the consequence of partaking of the forbidden fruit was physical death (see Genesis 2:17; Moses 3:17). Without our physical bodies, we could not possess or receive any of the promises of the covenant. Our physical bodies—created in the image of God—were essential to becoming like our heavenly parents in our divine natures and actions. Therefore, it became imperative for us to be restored to our physical bodies. So in the meridian of time, Jehovah would condescend to come to earth, receive a physical body from His mortal mother, retain "life in himself" (John 5:26) from His Heavenly Father, and break the bands of death for each one of us:

The death of Christ shall loose the bands of this temporal death, that all shall be raised from this temporal death.

The spirit and the body shall be reunited again in its perfect form; both limb and joint shall be restored to its proper frame, even as we now are at this time; and we shall be brought to stand before God, knowing even as we know now, and have a bright recollection of all our guilt.

Now, this restoration shall come to all, both old and young, both bond and free, both male and female, both the wicked and the righteous; and even there shall not so much as a hair of their heads be lost; but every thing shall be restored to its perfect frame, as it is now, or in the body, and shall be brought and be arraigned before the bar of Christ the Son, and God the Father, and the Holy Spirit, which is one Eternal God, to be judged according to their works, whether they be good or whether they be evil. (Alma 11:42–44)

The restoration of spirit to body shall come to every person who has ever lived upon this earth—unconditionally—because of Jesus Christ's victory over death through His Resurrection.

The second effect of the Fall overcome by the Atonement of Jesus Christ is sin. The Savior's Atonement—His suffering in Gethsemane and death on Calvary's cross—overcomes the effects of sin introduced by Adam and Eve by the Fall and makes us accountable for our own sins committed during mortality (see Mosiah 3:11); therefore, "men [and women] will be punished for their own sins and not for Adam's transgression" (Articles of Faith 1:2). The full effects of our collective sin would be borne by Jesus Christ in the meridian of time, including "the pains of all men, yea, the pains of every living creature, both men, women, and children, who belong to the family of Adam" (2 Nephi 9:21). His death on the cross would intensify the suffering experienced in Gethsemane[70] and seal His suffering with His blood. Jesus had to die to make His suffering complete and to execute the terms of Mediation according to the covenant.

Because of Him—the Mediator of the covenant, our Savior Jesus Christ—the two-fold effects of the Fall, even sin and death, can be overcome "to bring about the plan of mercy [and] appease the demands

---

70. See Russell M. Nelson, "The Correct Name of the Church," *Ensign* or *Liahona*, Nov. 2018, 88.

CHAPTER 5: THREE PILLARS OF ETERNITY

of justice, that God might be a perfect, just God, and a merciful God also" (Alma 42:15).

According to the demands of eternal justice, the restoration of body to spirit would require a restoration into God's presence to settle our individual accounts for the use of our agency during mortality. Such a restoration would condemn us because we would acknowledge—to our everlasting shame—that many of our choices were not aligned with the light within us and that we are guilty of sin or darkness. After all, a person cannot come into the light and not have their darkness exposed. The light of God's presence would be too much for us to bear, and "we would fain be glad if we could command the rocks and the mountains to fall upon us to hide us from his presence" (Alma 12:14). So our Father's plan of redemption appeases the demands of justice and provides us with mercy by ensuring that we cannot return to His presence until we have undergone the necessary transformation. Beginning with Adam and Eve, God placed safeguards—cherubim, or angels with a flaming sword—in the way of the tree of life so that they could not partake of that fruit and become immortal before they were ready, as Alma explained:

> And we see that death comes upon mankind . . . nevertheless there was a space granted unto man in which he might repent; therefore this life became a probationary state; a time to prepare to meet God; a time to prepare for that endless state . . . which is after the resurrection of the dead.
>
> Now, if it had not been for the plan of redemption, which was laid from the foundation of the world, there could have been no resurrection of the dead; but there was a plan of redemption laid, which shall bring to pass the resurrection of the dead, of which has been spoken. (Alma 12:24–25)

Jesus as our Mediator also becomes—through His atoning sacrifice—our great Testator of the new and everlasting covenant with the Father. The Greek word for covenant is *diatheke*, which among several notions also includes the idea of a will, the terms of which become effective when the testator dies (see Hebrews 9:16–17). Jesus, as our Testator, brings the terms of the covenant into effect because of His suffering and death for each of us. In effect, His death is a testament

73

that the terms of mercy required by the plan of salvation have been fulfilled. It was the idea of both a covenant and a testament that comes into effect only with death that defines the priestly ministry of Jesus.[71] This is what Abinadi meant when he testified to King Noah's court, "Yea, even so he shall be led, crucified, and slain. . . . Thus God breaketh the bands of death, having gained the victory over death; giving the Son power to make intercession for the children of men" (Mosiah 15:7–8). Jesus's death initiates the terms of the covenant and simultaneously conveys to Him the powers of intercession.

Why does a covenant only become efficacious upon the death of the victim, or testator? It is because our Father's covenant with us carries the assurance of eternal protection. Our Heavenly Father premortally covenanted with us that through His plan of redemption, we could live eternally and become like Him. That promise would have been frustrated once men inherited the conditions of death through the Fall of Adam and Eve unless our Father also provided the means to overcome the effects of the Fall—a plan of mercy—which He did through the offering of His Only Begotten Son (see John 3:16). When Jesus offered Himself as the perfect sacrifice for the cumulative effect of sin and death upon the world, the Father's covenantal assurance of eternal protection to us became guaranteed because Christ's payment to the demands of justice ensured that all men and women would live again, overcoming the effects of physical death.

Note also that the fulfillment of the terms of the covenant was "prepared, (or finished,) from the foundation of the world" (Joseph Smith Translation, Hebrews 4:3 [in Hebrews 4:3, footnote *a*]). Recall in Revelation 5 that the Lamb had been slain but arose and took the scroll from the hand of the Father, signifying the initiation of the plan of salvation. The Savior, from before the foundation of the world, set everything in motion: the Creation, the Fall, and the plan of redemption. His Atonement was infinite and eternal (see 2 Nephi 9:7; 25:16; Alma 34:10, 12), and it indicates that among the three pillars of

---

71. In Hebrews 9:15–17, Joseph Smith corrected the text to emphasize that the new covenant came into effect only with the death of a sacrificial victim— namely, the atoning death of Jesus Himself.

eternity—Creation, Fall, and Atonement—the Atonement occurred first, a staggering fact to comprehend.[72]

The Gospel of Jesus Christ

Jesus Christ offered His life as a ransom to the demands of justice and makes all mankind subject to Him, as their Creditor, for repayment (see 2 Nephi 9:5). As a condition for His mercy, Jesus Christ offers us His gospel as a pathway to experience the spiritual transformation to return again to the presence of our Heavenly Father. "The first principles and ordinances of the Gospel are: first, Faith in the Lord Jesus Christ; second, Repentance; third, Baptism by immersion for the remission of sins; fourth, Laying on of hands for the gift of the Holy Ghost" (Articles of Faith 1:4). The gospel of Jesus Christ would become the "everlasting covenant" to Adam and Eve and their posterity, "even that which was from the beginning" (Doctrine and Covenants 22:1), "to be a light to the world and a standard for [the Lord's] people" (Doctrine and Covenants 45:9). As Adam and Eve would come to learn for themselves, the gospel of Jesus Christ is inseparably linked with the Lord's character and nature and provides the necessary system to draw upon His power to transform their nature in preparation to their restoration into His presence at the Day of Judgment. The gospel of Jesus Christ is the plan of mercy within the new and everlasting covenant.

The gospel of Jesus Christ was revealed to Adam and Eve after their Fall and ensuing expulsion from the Garden of Eden. As discussed earlier, before they were driven from the garden, Adam and Eve were placed under covenant to obey certain select commandments and to offer sacrifices to the Lord. Interestingly, Adam and Eve did not know the full reason behind God's command to sacrifice the firstlings of their flocks to Him. Yet they were obedient "after many days" in fulfilling the commandment. In response to their obedience,

---

72. This is why prophets who lived before the coming of Jesus to the earth, like Abinadi, could speak of Christ's Atonement as though it had already occurred; "And now if Christ had not come into the world, speaking of things to come as though they had already come, there could have been no redemption" (Mosiah 16:6).

an angel came to teach them the purpose of the sacrificial offerings, asking Adam,

> Why dost thou offer sacrifices unto the Lord? And Adam said unto him: I know not, save the Lord commanded me.
>
> And then the angel spake, saying: This thing is a similitude of the sacrifice of the Only Begotten of the Father, which is full of grace and truth.
>
> Wherefore, thou shalt do all that thou doest in the name of the Son, and thou shalt repent and call upon God in the name of the Son forevermore.
>
> And in that day the Holy Ghost fell upon Adam, which beareth record of the Father and the Son, saying: I am the Only Begotten of the Father from the beginning, henceforth and forever, that as thou hast fallen thou mayest be redeemed, and all mankind, even as many as will. (Moses 5:7–9)

Adam and Eve learned that the price of redemption from their transgression in the garden would require obedience and sacrifice in similitude of the Only Begotten Son of God. The path forward would model Him in all things and would be a standard for them to live their lives.

As it is with us, the new and everlasting covenant was "new" to Adam and Eve because it was renewed with them again—this time in mortality. For us, it is "new" because it has been offered again in the dispensation of the fulness of times—or the last days preparatory to the Second Coming of Christ. It is the same covenant God made with Adam and Eve after the Fall and renewed through succeeding generations down until Moses, who was commanded to replace the covenant with a lesser law to prepare them to enter into God's presence.

Each person to whom the covenant is offered is required to receive it in order to realize the promised blessings the covenant ensures: "Verily I say unto you, blessed are you for receiving mine everlasting covenant, even the fulness of my gospel, sent forth unto the children of men, that they might have life and be made partakers of the glories which are to be revealed in the last days, as it was written by the prophets and apostles in days of old" (Doctrine and Covenants 66:2). Elder D. Todd Christofferson explains, "The scriptures speak of the new and everlasting covenant. The new and everlasting covenant is the gospel of Jesus Christ. In other words, the doctrines and commandments of the gospel constitute the substance of an everlasting covenant between God and man that is newly restored in each dispensation."[73]

Simply stated, the new and everlasting covenant reflects our premortal agreement with our Heavenly Father, and as it is revealed to us anew during mortality, it "is the sum total of all gospel covenants and obligations"[74] to prepare us in all things for the Final Judgment before God, which will evaluate what we have become in relation to our covenant promises and obligations. President Oaks explained, "The Final Judgment is not just an evaluation of a sum total of good and evil acts—what we have *done*. It is an acknowledgment of the final effect of our acts and thoughts—what we have *become*. It is not enough for anyone just to go through the motions. The commandments, ordinances, and covenants of the gospel are not a list of deposits required to be made in some heavenly account. The gospel of Jesus Christ is a plan that shows us how to become what our Heavenly Father desires us to become."[75]

The Abrahamic Covenant

According to the covenant they made with the Lord in the Garden of Eden, Adam and Eve taught their children the gospel (see Moses 5:12). For approximately two thousand years, the new and everlasting covenant was taught to the children of men with varying degrees of success down until the days of Abram, who was later renamed

---

73. D. Todd Christofferson, "The Power of Covenants," *Ensign* or *Liahona*, May 2009, 20.

74. Joseph Fielding Smith, *Doctrines of Salvation*, comp. Bruce R. McConkie (1955), 1:156.

75. Dallin H. Oaks, "The Challenge to Become," *Ensign*, Nov. 2000, 32. "The new and everlasting covenant is the fulness of the gospel of Jesus Christ. It includes all ordinances and covenants necessary for our salvation. It is 'new' whenever the Lord renews or restores it, and it is 'everlasting' because it does not change. . . . When you and I also enter that path, we have a new way of life. We thereby create a relationship with God that allows Him to bless and change us. The covenant path leads us back to Him. If we let God prevail in our lives, that covenant will lead us closer and closer to Him." Russell M. Nelson, "The Everlasting Covenant," *Liahona*, Oct. 2022, footnote 2 and paragraph 8.

Abraham[76] by the Lord after he received the covenant (see Joseph Smith Translation, Genesis 17:3–12; Genesis 17:1–12; Abraham 2:6, 8, 19; 3:11). As Adam received earlier, Abraham also received baptism, the priesthood, and eternal marriage—with Sarah his wife, specifically assuring them of an eternal increase in posterity.

Additionally, the Lord promised Abraham that the new and everlasting covenant would be offered to his posterity, and He indicated several specific blessings unique to him, namely that (1) Jesus Christ would be born through his lineage, and (2) Abraham's posterity would receive certain lands for an eternal inheritance, after the Resurrection. The same covenant offered to Abraham and Sarah was renewed with his son Issac and then Issac's son Jacob,[77] who received the new name of Israel at the time he received the covenant. Thus, all men and women who receive the same covenant become "the seed of Abraham" (Galatians 3:29; Doctrine and Covenants 84:35), members of the house of Israel, and heirs to the same promises. The promises made to Abraham and his seed are fully received in the Lord's house through the ordinance of marriage. Therefore, the ordinances of the gospel provide a spiritual birth into the covenantal promises the Lord first offered to Adam and Eve and that were renewed through Abraham and Sarah to their posterity and finally to us and all others who will receive them.

The covenantal relationship with God that we pursue when we receive the new and everlasting covenant anew in mortality matters so much to each of us. In order to make the association rich and rewarding to us, we must pursue a deeper comprehension of the conditions and obligations of the various ordinances of the covenant, which carry the potential to bind us and transform our various natures into new creatures in Christ. Unless we do this, "[we] can in nowise inherit the kingdom of God" (Moses 6:57).

---

76. *Abraham* means "father of a multitude" in Hebrew.

77. Bible Dictionary, "Abrahamic Covenant."

CHAPTER SUMMARY

1. Three pillars provide assurance that the plan of salvation will be fulfilled.

    a. The Creation
        i. The earth is our laboratory for testing within the new and everlasting covenant.
        ii. The earth was created spiritually before it was created physically.
        iii. The earth exercised its agency during the Creation.
        iv. The creation of the earth was a collective enterprise.
        v. The earth and its broader ecosystem are a miracle.

    b. The Fall of Adam and Eve
        i. Our Father created our bodies in His image with the breath of life.
        ii. The earth fell with Adam and Eve because Adam held dominion (priesthood keys) over it.
        iii. Adam and Eve are our models for testing in the new and everlasting covenant.
        iv. The conditions to honor agency were fashioned in the Garden of Eden.
        v. Jesus assumed the role of Mediator between us and our Father after the Fall of Adam and Eve.

    c. The Atonement of Jesus Christ
        i. The Atonement of Jesus Christ overcomes the effects of spiritual and physical death from the Fall of Adam and Eve.
        ii. The Atonement of Jesus Christ activates all of the activities of the plan of salvation, including the Resurrection and Final Judgment.

2. The gospel of Jesus Christ sets the conditions for the plan of redemption, or conditions to be applied on our behalf.

The New and Everlasting Covenant

a. The gospel of Jesus Christ offers all the necessary covenants and ordinances to inherit the promises of the new and everlasting covenant.

b. The Abrahamic covenant consists of the gospel of Jesus Christ and select promises made specifically to Abraham and his posterity.

Reflection Questions

- What aspects of the new and everlasting covenant stood out to you in this chapter?
- How do you show appreciation to God for this earth?
- What did you learn about Adam and Eve? How does your life compare to theirs?
- How is Jesus Christ our Mediator with our Heavenly Father? How does His Atonement enable such mediation?
- Who do you know who would benefit from what you have learned?

6

THE COVENANT RELATIONSHIP

A COVENANT RELATIONSHIP WITH THE LORD IS MEANT TO TRANS-form us. The purpose of providing specific conditions, obligations, and ordinances is to help us in our individual transformation by first defining and then "guaranteeing the future behavior of the partici-pant."[78] The metaphor of rebirth, or being born again, describes the nature of our designed transformation. The covenants we make with the Lord—if fulfilled by us—facilitate the rebirth and sanctification of our spirits to overcome the carnal, fallen natures we inherit from our physical birth in a telestial world (see Mosiah 27:25). The Lord promises to regenerate our spirits, to make us alive again, through the use of His body and blood—which He offered for us—on our behalf (see John 3:3–5; Moses 6:59).

We thus become His spirit sons and daughters through the or-dinances of His gospel and the ministration of the Holy Ghost (see Doctrine and Covenants 11:28–30; 25:1). We may, as Jesus did, assume the role of son or daughter as it is offered to us from the Father as we develop the character to receive it, but it does not come immediately.

---

78. Dale R. Renlund and Ruth L. Renlund, *The Melchizedek Priesthood: Understanding the Doctrine, Living the Principles* (Salt Lake City, UT: Deseret Book, 2018), 56.

As Elder David A. Bednar taught, "The spiritual rebirth . . . typically does not occur quickly or all at once; it is an ongoing process—not a single event. Line upon line and precept upon precept, gradually and almost imperceptibly, our motives, our thoughts, our words, and our deeds become aligned with the will of God. This phase of the transformation process requires time, persistence, and patience."[79]

Our spiritual rebirth into new, spiritual creatures—free from the desires for things temporary and evil—occurs by degrees as we apply the gospel of Jesus Christ in our lives, in time becoming His spirit sons and daughters.

The new and everlasting covenant is designed to facilitate a complete and perfect union between our Heavenly Father and us, His spirit sons and daughters—a union of minds, hearts, intentions, and behavior. The union fastens us to God, anchoring our spirits to His, making us "sure and steadfast, always abounding in good works" (Ether 12:4).[80] Though the covenant carries with it the promise of becoming joint heirs with Jesus Christ, it is not received upon equal footing with God. "It is important to notice," reads the Bible Dictionary, "that the two parties of the agreement do not stand in the relation of independent and equal contractors. God in His good pleasure fixes the terms, which [men and women] accept."[81] Our Heavenly Father gives us His word that the terms of the covenant—established before the foundation of the world (see Doctrine and Covenants 132:5)—will be confirmed as we meet them, a promise that gives us a perfect assurance because God's word, once spoken, must be fulfilled. As He has said, "For as I, the Lord God, liveth, even so my words cannot return void, for as they go forth out of my mouth they must be fulfilled" (Moses 4:30). We can trust God in our covenant relationship with Him. But

---

79. David A. Bednar, "Ye Must Be Born Again," *Ensign* or *Liahona*, May 2007, 21.

80. See David A. Bednar, "Be Still and Know That I Am God," *Liahona*, May 2024.

81. Bible Dictionary, "Covenant." "The gospel covenant is the promise of God to grant to man, through man's obedience and acceptance of the ordinances and principle of the gospel, the glory and exaltation of eternal life. It is the Father in Heaven who stipulates the terms of the covenant." Joseph Fielding Smith, *Doctrines of Salvation*, comp. Bruce R. McConkie (1955), 1:152.

Bilateral and Unilateral Covenants

The new and everlasting covenant is comprised of many covenants that have associated rights, laws, and ordinances that proscribe how they are received, how they are fulfilled, and how they are defined to make them operational in time and eternity. To fulfill the ultimate purpose of the new and everlasting covenant, God provides us with several preparatory covenants because through the making and keeping of covenants, we grow from grace to grace. This is because each ensuing covenant after the covenant of baptism contains additional responsibilities and authorities that expand upon the preceding covenant. Similarly, with each covenant we make with God, His promises to us likewise expand. Thus, we learn and grow by making and keeping a succession of bilateral covenants, and our promised inheritance, authority, and relationship with God expands. Our relationship changes as we successfully fulfill our obligations within the covenant; we mature from child to servant to friend, and ultimately to joint heirs with Christ.

Two forms of covenants exist within the new and everlasting covenant: unilateral and bilateral covenants. A unilateral covenant is an agreement that requires only one party to create a promise for an individual or group of people. For example, when you see a sign on a lamp post offering a monetary reward for the discovery and return of a lost cat, you are witnessing a unilateral contract. A single party provides a promise and specifies the required action to receive it. Though two or more parties participate in the agreement to fulfill the contract, only one party makes a promise. The other party is under no obligation to act. Even when you decide to look for the cat, find it, and return it to collect the reward, the contract remains unilateral because you made no commitment to the promisor that you would look for the cat. Your performance of the action is all that is needed to receive the reward. The presence of a promise to act is an essential difference between unilateral and bilateral contracts.

Bilateral covenants are different. In a bilateral contract, both participants make promises to one another. The terms of the contract do not have to be created together, but both parties must promise to the other to act in accordance with the offered terms. For example, I need my windows washed, inside and outside, without streaks, and by a certain date. These are the terms of the agreement, and they are terms that I establish. I promise to pay $500 for the service to be completed according to the terms, but in order to create a contract, I need to find another party who is also willing to promise to provide the services as outlined in the terms. So I advertise the terms, and an applicant calls me to learn more about the request. I promise to pay the applicant $500 once the actions are completed according to the terms, and the applicant promises to provide the service according to the terms. A bilateral agreement is now in force. Table 3 (below) summarizes the key aspects of unilateral and bilateral contracts.

	Unilateral	**Bilateral**
Parties Involved	One person or party	More than one party
Promise of Reward	Made only by the promisor	Both parties make promises to each other
Time Frame	Determined by the promisor	Both parties agree on the time frame for the service to be delivered

Table 3: Unilateral vs. Bilateral Contracts

Within the gospel of Jesus Christ, we participate in both unilateral and bilateral contracts. Some examples of unilateral contracts include the law of tithing, keeping the Sabbath day holy, and living the Word of Wisdom. These examples are unilateral contracts because the Lord has specified a set of rewards available to anyone who decides to act according to the terms. For instance, the Word of Wisdom is given as "a principle with a promise" to all "who are or can be called saints" (Doctrine and Covenants 89:3). And anyone who complies with the prescribed dietary terms, "who remember to keep and do these sayings, walking in obedience to the commandments, shall receive health in their navel, marrow to their bones . . . wisdom, great treasures of knowledge, even hidden treasures . . . shall run and not be weary, and walk and not faint, . . . and the destroying angel shall pass by them . . . and not slay them" (Doctrine and Covenants 89:18–21).

The bilateral contracts of the gospel plan are called covenants and are always coupled with the reception of an ordinance. Our Father has set the terms for receiving such ordinances. The covenants either are or will be available to everyone and are only received on an individual basis. For every ordinance, God reveals the terms and makes promises to us, and we in turn must make promises to Him to act according to the terms. As we accept and fulfill our obligations of gospel ordinances, our accountability toward God expands. We assume obligations to act according to the covenantal terms to qualify for associated promises. And in order to realize the fulness of the promises of the new and everlasting covenant, we must enter into a succession of bilateral contracts and keep their associated terms and conditions. The succession or series of covenants is also known as "the covenant path."[82]

The covenant path is progressive, meaning the ordinances build upon one another. The conditions (or laws), obligations, and ordinances progressively expand from one covenant and ordinance to the next, making the preceding conditions, obligations, and ordinances prerequisite to the reception of the next. This means that none of the laws of the gospel can be abandoned but must be perpetuated in our lives as we strive to become disciples of Christ. Similarly, one must observe the rites of every ordinance, meaning that in order for the ordinances to be recognized by God and ratified by the Holy Ghost, one must receive them in the prescribed form or manner. No one is authorized to perform or receive an ordinance outside of the revealed manner—no one. Therefore, no one can comply with the conditions of the covenant, nor assume the obligations completely, unless and until the ordinances are received exactly as prescribed by the Lord. In fact, various definitions of the word *ordinance* include (1) something ordained by Deity and (2) a prescribed act or ceremony.[83] "Will I accept of an offering, saith the Lord, that is not made in my name? Or

---

82. Dale G. Renlund, "Accessing God's Power through Covenants," *Liahona*, May 2023, 35.

83. *Merriam-Webster.com Dictionary*, s.v. "ordinance," accessed August 7, 2024, https://www.merriam-webster.com/dictionary/ordinance.

will I receive at your hands that which I have not appointed? And will I appoint unto you, saith the Lord, except it be by law, even as I and my Father ordained unto you, before the world was?" (Doctrine and Covenants 132:9–11)

Covenantal Conditions

Each bilateral covenant contains certain terms, or requirements, in order to be fulfilled. The terms serve as a type of measurement of godliness—terms that draw men and women toward the presence of God as they are satisfied. Therefore, the new and everlasting covenant is a standard that draws all men and women to God, a type of messenger that prepares everyone everywhere to meet God when He comes again: "And even so I have sent mine everlasting covenant into the world, to be a light to the world, and to be a standard for my people, and for the Gentiles to seek to it, and to be a messenger before my face to prepare the way before me" (Doctrine and Covenants 45:9).

Conditions of the new and everlasting covenant bring our entire system into a state of readiness to inherit promised blessings. Of necessity, the totality of our body, spirit, mind, and heart must be addressed, including the transformation of our physical bodies, the yielding of our hearts, the training of our minds, and the inclination of our spirits toward the things of eternity. The preparatory process not only affects *what* we learn but also *how* we learn. God has so arranged the conditions of the covenants to change how we think, what we feel, and how we behave.

Covenantal Obligations

When we covenant within the new and everlasting covenant, we are set apart to be distinct contributors to our Father's plan of salvation. "When men are called unto mine everlasting gospel, and covenant with an everlasting covenant, they are accounted as the salt of the earth and the savor of men" (Doctrine and Covenants 101:39). Thus, reception of the new and everlasting covenant obligates the receiver to take upon themselves the yoke of Jesus Christ, "following the example of the Son of the living God" (2 Nephi 31:16). One should not be surprised, therefore, that within the Church of Jesus Christ exist real obligations—obligations which both test and refine us into

Chapter 6: The Covenant Relationship

new creatures. It is through this covenantal relationship that we become even as He is, changing our very natures such that we obtain His mind, learn His will, and submit to all things whatsoever He sees fit to inflict upon us. As we assume and fulfill covenantal obligations, we are transformed.

Covenantal obligations exist for both parties within the new and everlasting covenant. That is, God assumes obligations as He extends covenants to us, and we assume obligations as we receive them. This occurs every time we enter into a bilateral contract with God. President Nelson explained this dynamic in this way:

> Obligations pertain to those who *give* and to those who *receive* ordinations or calls. . . . If I give keys to you, *I* have certain obligations, and *you* have certain obligations. For me as the giver, I have a duty toward your success. Should you fail, in a measure I have failed. So I must teach and train adequately to ensure your personal safety and, at the same time, safeguard precious property you are to use. For you as the receiver, obligations accompany the keys. You must know applicable laws and obey them. Loyalty is expected. And you should understand the power of your instrument. Obedience, loyalty, and understanding are implicit with your acceptance of those keys.[84]

Knowing that covenants with God involve obligations for both parties provides us with (1) assurance because God will uphold all of His promises to us; (2) motivation because we know that the associated promises are guaranteed as we fulfill our obligations; and (3) responsibility because we are clear of our required behaviors within the agreement. Knowledge of our obligations leads us "to act and not [remain] to be acted upon" (2 Nephi 2:14). And oh, how our Father wants us to know and understand His covenants and the associated obligations and promises! President Nelson so testified: "He is the One who wants you to understand with great clarity exactly what you are making covenants to do. He is the One who wants you to experience fully His sacred ordinances. He wants you to comprehend

---

84. Russell M. Nelson, "Keys of the Priesthood," *Ensign*, Nov. 1987, 37.

your privileges, promises, and responsibilities. He wants you to have spiritual insights and awakenings you've never had before."[85]

Several years ago, I was in a discussion with a friend at work, and the topic turned to his challenges outside of work. He was in a leadership position for his church, and their pastor and leadership team were struggling to know whether they should spend the little money they had to replace the roof of one of their church buildings. He inquired of me about our church and whether we faced similar challenges. I explained that we did not because all of our donations were centralized and capital expenditures for buildings were managed separately. I asked him if his congregation lived the law of tithing; he said that they did not and that very few members of the congregation gave offerings to the church. This led me to inquire about what he and other members of their congregation believed about their baptisms. He replied that they believed it was a commandment to be baptized and that it symbolized their belief in Jesus Christ and carried blessings from God. I asked if they considered it to be a covenant with God, with reciprocal obligations between them and God. He replied, "Well, that's the issue—that is it, right there."

What my friend meant was that their belief in baptism did not obligate them to act. Rather, it was for them a unilateral covenant with no promise from the receiver toward God. Thus, baptism did not obligate their members to give, but if they chose to do so, they would be blessed. Certainly, their members did not collectively feel constrained to give their means to replace the roof, so it was left to a few. What they lacked was the motivating power of obligations within a bilateral covenant.

In addition to the motivating power of bilateral covenant obligations, our individual reception of covenants permits us to grow in learning how to access priesthood power. It is through the covenants and ordinances of the priesthood that we ultimately arrive at the point the scriptures describe as holding "the keys of all the spiritual blessings of the church" (Doctrine and Covenants 107:18). All those who hold this holy order "have the privilege of receiving the mysteries of

---

85. Russell M. Nelson, "The Temple and Your Spiritual Foundation," *Ensign* or *Liahona*, Nov. 2021, 95.

the kingdom of heaven, to have the heavens opened unto them, to commune with the general assembly and church of the Firstborn, and to enjoy the communion and presence of God the Father, and Jesus the mediator of the new covenant" (Doctrine and Covenants 107:19).

This transformational journey begins with the bilateral covenants of the gospel of Jesus Christ and by assuming our obligations within the covenant. As Elder Dale G. Renlund explains it: "Before the earth was created, God established covenants as the mechanism by which we, His children, could unite ourselves to Him. Based on eternal, unchanging law, He specified the nonnegotiable conditions whereby we are transformed, saved, and exalted. In this life, we make these covenants by participating in priesthood ordinances and promising to do what God asks us to do, and in return, God promises us certain blessings."[86]

COVENANTAL ORDINANCES

Covenantal ordinances, also known as saving ordinances, are central in the ongoing process of spiritual rebirth and transformation. The gospel of Jesus Christ has many ordinances, but not all are considered necessary for our spiritual transformation or final exaltation.[87] Saving ordinances require a bilateral agreement with God. One way to distinguish a saving ordinance from other gospel ordinances is whether it is performed on behalf of the dead in holy temples. If it is done on behalf of the living *and* the dead, it is essential for salvation.[88]

The saving ordinances a person must receive are few, consisting of baptism, confirmation (receiving the gift of the Holy Ghost), conferral

---

86. Dale G. Renlund, "Accessing God's Power through Covenants," 35.

87. *General Handbook: Serving in The Church of Jesus Christ of Latter-day Saints,* 18.1, Gospel Library.

88. One ordinance often considered a saving ordinance, but is not, is the ordinance of the sacrament. The purpose of the sacrament is to remember and renew the covenantal promises we have already received. We do not accept or promise to make any new obligation when we partake of the sacrament; therefore, the purpose of the sacrament is solely for the living and not the dead. The sacrament, as is the case with other non-saving ordinances, is a channel "to receive [God's] power, healing, comfort, and guidance." *General Handbook,* 18.2.

of the Melchizedek Priesthood (for men), the temple endowment (a package of covenants and ordinances received in succession to one another), and the temple sealing (or marriage). As is the case with all bilateral covenants, each carries its own obligations and promises. When received and fulfilled in total, the promises equate to an inheritance in the highest degree of the celestial kingdom of God (see chapter 3 of this book). In other words, in order to receive the highest blessings of the new and everlasting covenant, a person must receive all ordinances of salvation and fulfill the associated obligations (see Doctrine and Covenants 132:6). It is the same path revealed to Adam and Eve and constitutes the strait and narrow path leading to God's presence.

All of the saving ordinances must be performed in the manner revealed by God and by His authority, namely the priesthood. In addition to these general conditions, there are specific conditions related to the covenant for each ordinance that must be met before the covenantal promises can take effect in the life of the recipient. The Holy Ghost, the third member of the Godhead "who knoweth all things" (Moses 6:61), has the responsibility to fulfill the promises of the covenant by providing His seal of approval when the conditions are met (see Doctrine and Covenants 132:7). This ensures that no one can partake of the promises unworthily, because God will not be mocked. Table 4 summarizes the conditions, obligations, and promises associated with the ordinances of the gospel of Jesus Christ.

BAPTISM

Baptism is the first ordinance of the gospel of Jesus Christ. It is the gate by which a person enters the covenant path. Furthermore, it is a sign to God of our willingness to take His name upon us and to keep His commandments. The authorized mode of baptism is by immersion, as has been revealed (see 3 Nephi 11:23–27; Doctrine and Covenants 20:72–74) and as the name in Greek implies ("to dip or immerse" in water). It is performed by a man who has had the priesthood conferred upon him, holds the office of priest or elder within the priesthood, and is authorized by a presiding authority with priesthood keys, usually a bishop.

CHAPTER 6: THE COVENANT RELATIONSHIP

	Conditions	Obligations	Promises
Baptism[89]	• Be accountable before God for individual sins • Exercise faith in Jesus Christ • Repent of your sins[90] • Have a desire to be baptized	• Humble yourself before God • Take upon yourself the name of Jesus Christ • Obey His commandments • Endure valiantly to the end	• Open a channel for the reception of the Holy Ghost[91] • Enter the strait and narrow path to the celestial kingdom (born of water)
Confirmation[92] (Gift Of the Holy Ghost)	• Receive baptism • Offer a broken heart and contrite spirit • Manifest by works the reception of the Spirit of Christ (no hypocrisy, no deception, real intent)	Receive the Holy Ghost by: • Being willing to take the name of Jesus Christ • Always remembering the Son • Keeping the commandments of God	• Receive a remission of sins • Become a member of The Church of Jesus Christ of Latter-Day Saints • Begin the path to personal sanctification (born of the spirit) • Have the constant companionship of the Holy Ghost

---

89. See 2 Nephi 31:18–20; Mosiah 18:8–10; Alma 7:15; Doctrine and Covenants 20:37.

90. The Hebrew word for *repentance* is *Teshuva*, which consists of three root words: *Tav, Shin*, and *Vaw. Tav* represents a covenant, *shin* represents jagged teeth or devouring, and *vaw* represents a home. Interpreted together, the meaning is to make a covenant that you will devour your sins in order to return home. Baptism is the associated ordinance with the covenant to repent.

91. *The Joseph Smith Papers, Documents, Volume 6: June 26–August 4, 1839*, 523.

92. See 2 Nephi 31:13; Doctrine and Covenants 20:77, 79; Dallin H. Oaks, "Taking upon Us the Name of Jesus Christ," *Ensign*, May 1985.

Melchizedek Priesthood[93]	• Receive baptism and confirmation • Receive priesthood ordination (men)	Receive the priesthood by: • Magnifying your calling • Being cautious of your own self • Diligently heeding the word of God • Living by every word of God • Leading by persuasion, long-suffering, gentleness, meekness, love unfeigned, kindness, and pure knowledge	• Be sanctified by the Spirit • Have their bodies renewed • Become the seed of Abraham, the sons of Moses and Aaron (men), the Church and kingdom, and the elect of God • Receive the Lord and the Father • Receive the Father's kingdom • Become clean from the blood and sins of this generation
Temple Endowment[94]	• Receive baptism and confirmation • Receive priesthood ordination first (men) • Washed (preparatory) • Anointed (symbolically) • Clothed (physically) • Given a new name	• Demonstrate exactness and honor in keeping covenants • Wear the garment as instructed throughout life • Hold sacred certain information to enter the Father's presence • Obedience • Sacrifice • The doctrine of Christ • Chastity • Consecration • Love God and fellowmen	• Be cleansed from the sins of this generation (women) • Be shielded and protected from Satan's devices • Gain knowledge of the plan of salvation • Be endowed with spiritual power from on high • Obtain knowledge to enter the Father's presence

93. See Doctrine and Covenants 84:33–44; 121:41–42; Jacob 1:19.

94. See Exodus 29:4–9; *General Handbook*, 27.2; Alma 57:21; Doctrine and Covenants 38:32, 38; 43:16; Carlos E. Asay, C. "The Temple Garment: An Outward Expression of an Inward Commitment," *Ensign*, Aug. 1997.

Temple Marriage[95] (Patriarchal Priesthood)	• Receive the temple endowment	Receive the other by: • Cleaving unto each other • Counseling together • Laboring together • Fulfilling appointed roles as father and mother • Presiding in righteousness • Being willing to bear children • Teaching their children the gospel	• Experience the patriarchal priesthood • Obtain the blessings of Abraham, Issac, and Jacob • Rise in the morning of the First Resurrection • Be given thrones, kingdoms, principalities, powers, dominions, and exaltations • Have your name written in the Lamb's Book of Life • Experience a fulness and continuation of endless posterity
Cleansing and Coronation[96] (Second Anointing)	• Receive temple marriage • Sealed by the Holy Spirit of Promise.	• Love and serve God with all heart, might, mind, and strength (unweariingness) • Overcome by faith • Be valiant in the testimony of Jesus • Become as a little child	• Receive the fulness of the priesthood • Be sealed with the Father's seal of the new and everlasting covenant • Have the Holy Ghost as a constant companion • Become a king and priest (man) or queen and priestess (woman) • Experience the administration of the Second Comforter

Table 4: Covenant Path of the Gospel of Jesus Christ

---

95. See Genesis 2:24; 2 Nephi 2:20; Doctrine and Covenants 42:22; 68:25; 132:19; Moses 5:1–12; "The Family: A Proclamation to the World," Gospel Library; see also Russell M. Nelson, "Lessons from Eve," *Ensign*, Nov. 1987.

96. See Mosiah 3:19; Helaman 10:4–7; 3 Nephi 11:35–38; Doctrine and Covenants 76:53; 121:29.

When we are baptized, we witness our willingness to take upon ourselves the name of Jesus Christ and keep His commandments to the end of our lives, acting sincerely as we so do. To be baptized without a sincere heart or real intent to follow the Savior's gospel is to take the name of the Lord in vain, something we are expressly forbidden to do (see Exodus 20:7; Doctrine and Covenants 136:21). Elder Renlund explains:

> In this context, let us be mindful of the Old Testament commandment, "Thou shalt not take the name of the Lord thy God in vain." To our modern ears, this sounds like a prohibition against irreverently using the Lord's name. The commandment includes that, but its injunction is even more profound. The Hebrew word translated as "take" means to "lift up" or "carry," as one would a banner that identifies oneself with an individual or group. The word translated as "vain" means "empty" or "deceptive." The commandment to not take the Lord's name in vain can thus mean, "You should not identify yourself as a disciple of Jesus Christ unless you intend to represent Him well."[97]

For those who sincerely repent and are baptized, the Lord promises two specific beginnings: first, the assurance that they have entered the covenant path and will be saved, and second, the beginning of spiritual rebirth, having been born of water. This initial symbolic cleansing promises a fulfillment through the second part of baptism, confirmation, where the remission of their sins and their membership in the kingdom of God will be verified. It foretells their future death and resurrection from the dead through their immersion or burial in the water and coming up again from the water into a kingdom of glory.

CONFIRMATION

The second part of baptism is confirmation through the laying on of hands. It is received by a Melchizedek Priesthood holder and authorized by a presiding priesthood authority, usually a bishop. The person performing the ordinance is obligated to pronounce two blessings upon the recipient; first, the person is confirmed a member of The

---

97. Dale G. Renlund, "Accessing God's Power through Covenants," 36.

Chapter 6: The Covenant Relationship

Church of Jesus Christ of Latter-day Saints, and second, the person is commanded to "receive the Holy Ghost" (Doctrine and Covenants 20:41). Notably, the Holy Ghost is not told to go to the person, but the person is commanded to receive it, thereby ensuring that the blessings and gifts of the Holy Ghost cannot be received unworthily. If the recipient sincerely offers a broken heart and contrite spirit and has demonstrated by their works that they have repented of their sins through keeping the commandments, then the promise of God in the covenant is that their sins will be remitted through the administration of the Holy Ghost or baptism of fire. And as long as the member continually strives to keep the commandments of God, continually repenting of their sins and improving, the promise is that the Holy Ghost will always be with them to teach, warn, comfort, guide, and protect. The Holy Ghost serves as an accelerant down the covenant path.

Priesthood Ordination (Men)

All covenants and ordinances belong to the holy priesthood. Therefore, all who receive priesthood covenants and ordinances possess the right to wield priesthood authority and power in their lives and assignments in the Church under the direction of presiding officers who hold priesthood keys. Thus, the oath and covenant of the priesthood extends blessings to both men and women equally. However, we tend—historically—to associate the term "oath and covenant of the priesthood" only with men who are ordained to a priesthood office. In the context of the new and everlasting covenant, this association does not make a lot of sense.

The Lord has not revealed why only men are ordained to priesthood offices. Elder Neal A. Maxwell explained, "We know so little . . . about the reasons for the division of duties between womanhood and manhood as well as between motherhood and priesthood. These were divinely determined in another time and another place."[98] What we do know is that men and women are asked to do some unique tasks in building the kingdom of God, both within the family and in the Church, and all tasks are meant to be mutually reinforcing. Why is it

---

98. Neal A. Maxwell, "The Women of God," *Ensign*, May 1978, 10.

that, along the covenant path, men require priesthood ordination and women do not? Why do women receive some blessings unconditionally while the promises are conditional for men?

The answer to such questions is that we simply do not know. When viewing the obligations and promises associated with the oath and covenant of the priesthood, however, we see that they are almost entirely the same for both men and women. Both are obligated to magnify callings—all callings within the new and everlasting covenant are priesthood callings—and to live by every word of God. Each is required to beware of themselves and give diligent heed to the words of eternal life. And it is through the power of the priesthood and the reception of the ordinances thereof that both men and women are sanctified by the Spirit, their bodies are renewed,[99] and they qualify for entrance into the Church and kingdom of God. Likewise, it is through priesthood ordinances that both men and women are cleansed from the blood and sins of this generation, though the reception of such blessing comes earlier to women than men.

When the priesthood covenant speaks of magnifying a calling, it is better understood in the context of grace (as explained in 2 Nephi 25:23) than pure ingenuity or effort. This is because our best efforts, though essential, are not equivalent, nor are they sufficient. "After all that we can do" should suggest to us that our best efforts to magnify will fall short and must be lifted up by God to find the mark. We simply cannot serve perfectly to meet the known—let alone hidden— needs of those around us. We all need help from the Holy Ghost, which is a function of God's grace in our lives. We must learn to serve by inviting the Holy Ghost into our service (which represents the will of the Lord) and then do all we can in yielding to his enticings. This pattern is the process of becoming a saint and stripping off the natural man.

---

99. The renewing of the body is one way Jesus Christ strengthens us when we are spent. The term *renew* carries several meanings relevant to the Savior's approach to strengthening us: (1) resume an activity; (2) reestablish a relationship; (3) repeat an activity; (4) provide fresh life, strength, or revive; (5) extend for a further period a contract or license; and (6) replace something worn out. The Savior gives us power to do all of these as circumstances require.

CHAPTER 6: THE COVENANT RELATIONSHIP

TEMPLE ENDOWMENT

The temple endowment is a package of covenants and ordinances experienced in succession. It is best thought of in two parts: (1) preparatory or initiatory ordinances and (2) knowledge and instruction ordinances. The initiatory ordinances consist of three parts: washing, anointing, and clothing. To be prepared along the covenant path to prevail against the adversary, we must be built upon the rock of Jesus Christ (see Helaman 5:20), from the top of our heads to the soles of our feet. The purpose of the ordinances of washing and anointing our bodies is to prepare us in all things for such challenges. The entire body must be cleansed and armed with the Holy Ghost to discern between truth and error and to fight valiantly. In addition, our spirits need help to become "new creatures" with hearts and minds that can hear God's voice and withstand temptations that may beset us. We must be prepared for the difficulties to come in marriage and raising children in a fallen world. We need strength to draw upon the Savior when our hands hang down and our knees become feeble (see Doctrine and Covenants 81:5). In short, we need the promise of the Father of "renew[ed] strength; they shall mount up with wings as eagles; they shall run, and not be weary; and they shall walk, and not faint" (Isaiah 40:31).

The washing, anointing, and clothing elements of the initiatory provide such protection according to the faithfulness of the recipient in honoring the obligations of the covenant. In short, they restore light to the recipient, as was the case with Adam and Eve. The concluding gift of the initiatory is a garment of light that serves as a constant reminder of covenantal obligations to God. Failure to live up to one's covenants leaves the recipient vulnerable to the power of the devil and his attempts to chain them down to destruction (see Alma 12:6), and they are left without "a cloak" (John 15:22) to cover their nakedness before God.

The knowledge and instruction portions of the endowment provide the recipient with the information needed to enter into the Father's presence and with a succession of covenants to accelerate their spiritual transformation. Speaking of the knowledge portion of the endowment, President Brigham Young explained, "Your endowment is, to receive all those ordinances in the house of the Lord, which are necessary for you, after you have departed this life, to enable you to walk back to the presence of the Father, passing the angels who stand as sentinels."[100]

The knowledge portion of the endowment enables a person to progress "back to the presence of the Father, passing the angels who stand as sentinels." But the information provided is not meant to be solely memorized. Rather, it should be embodied. It is through the embodiment of the information that a person's character is altered to be worthy of entrance into the presence of the Father, and the Holy Ghost must seal it as such. Proof that the covenant is active in our lives can be found when we identify with the requirements such that our thoughts, actions, and feelings are governed by them.

When Adam and Eve were first driven from the Garden of Eden—from the presence of the Lord—the Father directed Jehovah to place angels with a flaming sword to guard the way back to the tree of life. The angels were sentinels, or protectors of the path back to God's presence, to prevent any unprepared entrants from partaking of the fruit and living forever in their sins (see Moses 4:28–31). Anyone who has been prepared (transformed) by priesthood covenants can pass the angels, but they first must come to embody what the covenants enable.

In addition to their spiritual transformation, additional information is needed to prepare. The first piece of information is the reception of a new name.

Similar to other prototypes who received a new name associated with the reception of ordinances of the new and everlasting covenant, the recipient also receives a new name in connection with the temple endowment. Recall from chapter 3 that those who enter into the presence of the Father receive a white stone with a new name written upon it that is only known to the recipient (see Doctrine and Covenants 130:8–11). It is during the temple endowment that the new name is communicated. The recipient is obligated to not divulge the name but to remember it and safeguard it for later use. After one has been necessarily prepared through the initiatory ordinances, they are prepared for further light and knowledge in the endowment ordinances.

---

100. *Teachings of Presidents of the Church: Brigham Young* (1997), 302.

CHAPTER 6: THE COVENANT RELATIONSHIP

The next portion of knowledge received during the endowment consists of the reception of five successive covenants and ordinances, the obligations of which include the reception of the laws of obedience, sacrifice, the gospel of Jesus Christ (or doctrine of Christ), chastity, and consecration.[101] Elder Renlund described the laws as follows:

> In the endowment, we covenant, first, to strive to keep the commandments of God; second, to repent with a broken heart and contrite spirit; third, to live the gospel of Jesus Christ. We do this by exercising faith in Him, making covenants with God as we receive the ordinances of salvation and exaltation, keeping those covenants throughout our lives, and striving to live the two great commandments to love God and neighbor. We covenant, fourth, to keep the law of chastity and, fifth, to dedicate ourselves and everything the Lord blesses us with to build up His Church. . . .
>
> As you come to Christ and are connected to Him and our Heavenly Father by covenant, something seemingly unnatural happens. You are transformed and become perfected in Jesus Christ. You become a covenant child of God and an inheritor in His kingdom.[102]

In addition to what Elder Renlund described of the covenants made, the *General Handbook* provides the following explanations of the obligations for each covenant:

1. Live the law of obedience and strive to keep Heavenly Father's commandments.
2. Obey the law of sacrifice, which means sacrificing to support the Lord's work and repenting with a broken heart and contrite spirit.
3. Obey the law of the gospel of Jesus Christ, which means:
   a. Exercising faith in Jesus Christ.
   b. Repenting daily.
   c. Making covenants with God by receiving the ordinances of salvation and exaltation.
   d. Enduring to the end by keeping covenants.

---

101. See *General Handbook*, 27.2.

102. Dale G. Renlund, "Accessing God's Power through Covenants," 36–43.

The New and Everlasting Covenant

    e.   Striving to live the two great commandments. These are to "love the Lord thy God with all thy heart, and with all thy soul, and with all thy mind" and to "love thy neighbor as thyself" (Matthew 22:37, 39).

4.   Keep the law of chastity, which means abstaining from sexual relations outside of a legal marriage between a man and a woman, which is according to God's law.

5.   Keep the law of consecration, which means that members dedicate their time, talents, and everything with which the Lord has blessed them to building up Jesus Christ's Church on the earth.[103]

Connected with the covenants and obligations of the endowment are the promises of the Lord that we will know about His plan of salvation, receive power from on high, and know how to enter again into His presence. It is through the combination of preparatory ordinances and the reception of additional covenants with God that we leave the temple endowed with knowledge of the new and everlasting covenant offered to mankind and where it leads (explained for the first time in a single telling). It is in the temple that we accept specific obligations to answer the Savior's question more completely in our lives: "What manner of men ought ye to be? (3 Nephi 27:27).

One author commented on the focused nature of the covenants of the temple endowment:

> We have noted that the covenants of the endowment are progressively more binding, in the sense of allowing less and less latitude for personal interpretation as one advances. Thus, 1) the law of God is general and mentions no specifics; 2) the law of obedience states that specific orders are to be given and observed; 3) the law of sacrifice still allows a margin of interpretation; 4) the law of chastity, on the other hand, is something else; here at last we have an absolute, bound by a solemn sign; 5) finally the law of consecration is equally

---

103. *General Handbook*, 27.2.

CHAPTER 6: THE COVENANT RELATIONSHIP

uncompromising, everything the Lord has given one is to be consecrated. This law is bound by the firmest token of all.[104]

Through the temple endowment, our individual preparation culminates, and we are prepared for the next covenantal obligation, one that requires us to work together unlike anything before, even the covenant of marriage—an institution and relationship that in our world has increasingly become a stumbling block to many. As the Lord told Joseph Smith, "For strait is the gate, and narrow the way that leadeth unto the exaltation and continuation of the lives, and few there be that find it, because ye receive me not in the world neither do ye know me" (Doctrine and Covenants 132:22).

MARRIAGE (PATRIARCHAL PRIESTHOOD)

In 1843, less than a year before his death, the Prophet Joseph Smith spoke to the Saints about three grand orders of the priesthood, namely the Melchizedek, patriarchal, and Aaronic. Referring to the patriarchal priesthood, the Prophet said, "Go to and finish the temple, and God will fill it with power, and you will then receive more knowledge concerning this Priesthood."[105] The patriarchal priesthood is received through the new and everlasting covenant of marriage (see Doctrine and Covenants 131:2), or temple marriage. It is called the patriarchal priesthood because it is in this ordinance that men and women are authorized to create families, rear them in righteousness, and receive all blessings promised to the great patriarchs Abraham, Issac, and Jacob. Speaking of this pattern, Elder Bruce R. McConkie explained, "We can enter an order of the priesthood named the new and everlasting covenant of marriage, named also the patriarchal order, because of which order we can create for ourselves eternal family units of our own, patterned after the family of God our Heavenly Father."[106]

---

104. Hugh Nibley, *Approaching Zion* (Salt Lake City, UT: Deseret Book, 1989), 424.

105. History, 1838–1856, volume E-1 [1 July 1843–30 April 1844], 1708, josephsmithpapers.org.

106. Bruce R. McConkie, "The Doctrine of the Priesthood," *Ensign*, May 1982, 34.

The patriarchal priesthood was handed down anciently from the Father to His righteous sons (see Doctrine and Covenants 107:39–56). It is an order of priesthood that seeks to make two people as one through increased physical and spiritual unity. Men and women in this order are commanded to "cleave unto" the other and to give themselves to each other, becoming one flesh. They come together physically to create children who are two equal halves of the mother and father, living symbols of the commandment to become one. They are, within this priesthood order, commanded to fulfill their divinely appointed duties as husband and wife, father and mother, and to lead their posterity in righteousness after the example of Jesus Christ. Children born to men and women who have received this ordinance are entitled to inherit all of the same blessings of their parents, possessing and receiving all of the blessings of the covenant because their parents will—in order to fulfill their covenantal obligations—teach them the gospel in their youth (see Doctrine and Covenants 68:25).

Today, the Church today is not organized and led patriarchally. Instead, offices within the Melchizedek Priesthood, such as elder, high priest, patriarch, Seventy, and Apostle direct the organization of the Church generally and through various areas, stakes, and wards throughout the world. However, every husband and wife who has been married according to God's law in the holy temple leads their family after the patriarchal order. In the highest degree of the celestial kingdom, the patriarchal order will be the order of the day, with husbands and wives filling their roles as kings and queens, priests and priestesses, to their posterity.[107]

Temple marriage is received within dedicated temples at temple altars where the ceremony is presided over and performed by temple sealers—Melchizedek Priesthood holders who have been authorized and have had the sealing power conferred upon them by the President of the Church or his designee. The ceremony is relatively brief. Men and women covenant with God and receive obligations to serve, counsel, and cleave to one another, which means to give their absolute loyalty and devotion to each other and to none else. Thus, they are obligated to each other through a horizontal connection. Additionally,

---

107. Bruce R. McConkie, *Mormon Doctrine*, 2nd ed. (1966), 559.

CHAPTER 6: THE COVENANT RELATIONSHIP

through the ordinance, couples enter into a vertical relationship with the Lord to create an eternal family unit and to rear children in love and righteousness.[108] No greater responsibility is granted to men and women in the new and everlasting covenant than that offered in temple marriage.

Because the responsibilities of temple marriage are so profound, so too are the associated promises. Fulfilling the terms of the covenant carries the promise of a glorious Resurrection—even the First Resurrection, the promise of eternal inheritance, endless posterity, and life with our heavenly parents and Savior Jesus Christ in the highest degree of the celestial kingdom (see Doctrine and Covenants 131:1–2). Couples' names are written in the Lamb's book of life (see Alma 5:58). Doctrine and Covenants 132 further explains:

> It shall be done unto them in all things whatsoever my servant hath put upon them, in time, and through all eternity; and shall be of full force when they are out of the world; and they shall pass by the angels, and the gods, which are set there, to their exaltation and glory in all things, as hath been sealed upon their heads, which glory shall be a fulness and a continuation of the seeds forever and ever.
>
> Then shall they be gods, because they have no end; therefore shall they be from everlasting to everlasting, because they continue; then shall they be above all, because all things are subject unto them. Then shall they be gods, because they have all power, and the angels are subject unto them. (Doctrine and Covenants 132:19–20)

There are no higher blessings promised than those associated with eternal marriage!

Unfortunately, for many who have received temple marriage, the thought of such promises is not a happy one. Some feel that their marriage, though one or both have kept their covenantal obligations, has not met the "oneness" requirement within the union. For persons in such relationships as these, President Oaks has taught, "We have a loving Heavenly Father who will see that we receive every blessing and every advantage that our own desires and choices allow. We also know

---

108. See Russell M. Nelson, *Heart of the Matter: What 100 Years of Living Have Taught Me* (Salt Lake City, UT: Deseret Book, 2023), chapter 6.

that He will force no one into a sealing relationship against his or her will. The blessings of a sealed relationship are assured for all who keep their covenants but never by forcing a sealed relationship on another person who is unworthy or unwilling."[109]

In the next life, no one will be caught in a situation where the desires of their hearts are not honored. This includes situations where only one partner has been true to their temple marriage obligations, situations where both partners have been loyal but not grown together as one, and any other scenario in between.

What is also clear is that no one will be forced to marry eternally, and there will be many who will be content remaining separate and single in the celestial kingdom. Such individuals "are appointed angels in heaven, which angels are ministering servants, to minister for those who are worthy of a far more, and an exceeding, and an eternal weight of glory. For these angels did not abide my law; therefore, they cannot be enlarged, but remain separately and singly, without exaltation, in their saved condition, to all eternity; and from henceforth are not gods, but are angels of God forever and ever" (Doctrine and Covenants 132:16–17). Those who wish to "remain separately and singly, without exaltation" will have knowingly chosen it. Everyone who really wants to live a celestial law at the highest degree will have the opportunity, but there will be, apparently, some who will remain "ministering servants" and will be happy doing so.

One final point of emphasis is needed in regard to temple marriage. Everyone who desires it will ultimately receive it. Many men and women have longed for the companionship and blessings of the covenant of temple marriage and have not received it in mortality. However, the covenant of the Father to us from before the foundation of the world is that the promises of temple marriage will be extended to all those with "desires to serve God" who "serve him with all [their] heart, mind, might and strength" (Doctrine and Covenants 4:2–3). The commandment to "ask, and ye shall receive; knock, and it shall be opened unto you" (3 Nephi 27:29; Doctrine and Covenants 4:7) shall find fulfillment through the promises of temple marriage. On this topic, Elder Neil L. Anderson promised:

---

109. Dallin H. Oaks, "Kingdoms of Glory," *Liahona*, Nov. 2023, 29.

We cannot always explain the difficulties of our mortality. Sometimes life seems very unfair—especially when our greatest desire is to do exactly what the Lord has commanded. As the Lord's servant, I assure you that this promise is certain: "Faithful members whose circumstances do not allow them to receive the blessings of eternal marriage and parenthood in this life will receive all promised blessings in the eternities, [as] they keep the covenants they have made with God."[110]

CLEANSING AND CORONATION

In the temple endowment, we are washed and anointed preparatory to becoming a king and priest or queen and priestess unto the Most High God (El-Elyon), meaning our Heavenly Father. The final ordinance to receive, though not necessarily in this life, is the capstone ordinance of cleansing and coronation—a second anointing as a king and priest, queen and priestess, unto the Most High God, to rule and reign over our inherited kingdoms forever. This ordinance pronounces the recipient clean from the blood and sins of this generation and confers the fulness of the Melchizedek Priesthood, enabling the couple to administer both ecclesiastically and autocratically over their posterity in eternity and endowing them with the right to ask and receive, and to knock and have the heavens opened unto them. This ordinance is typically preceded by receiving one's calling and election, or the assurance of eternal life from the Holy Ghost, through revelation and the spirit of prophecy (see Doctrine and Covenants 131:5–6).

The ordinance is performed in the temple at the direction of the President of the Church for both husband and wife. Though performed less regularly than in the early days of the Restoration, the ordinance is still performed on occasion.[111] Though this ordinance will ultimately be received by all faithful couples, prophets and apostles have emphasized that it's not necessary to receive this ordinance in mortality to receive the fulness of covenantal promises. This is because the fulness of the promises is received through temple marriage,

---

110. Neil A. Anderson, "Children," *Ensign* or *Liahona*, Nov. 2011, 30.

111. See Russell M. Nelson, *From Heart to Heart: An Autobiography* (Concord, NH: Quality Press, 1979), 359–60.

whereas this ordinance provides the realization of such blessings, according to the couple's faithfulness, in essence fulfilling the terms of the agreement.

The blessing of receiving one's calling and election can occur individually but must ultimately be received as a couple. This is because only husbands and wives sealed together by the Holy Spirit of Promise inherit the fulness of promises within the new and everlasting covenant. The knowledge of one's calling and election can occur before the reception of the ordinance. It is given by God to the recipients in acknowledgment of their willingness to serve Him at all costs, where the couple has demonstrated their resolve to "overcome by faith" (Doctrine and Covenants 76:53) and through the sacrifice of all things.[112] "Wherefore," says Nephi, "if ye shall press forward, feasting upon the word of Christ, and endure to the end, behold, thus saith the Father: Ye shall have eternal life" (2 Nephi 31:20). The reception of such knowledge is sacred and deeply personal, so one would not expect to hear about these experiences in public. The pursuit of such an assurance from God is a blessing of discipleship, however, and as such, it should be pursued "with all our heart, might, mind, and strength."

Speaking of the new and everlasting covenant as conditions, obligations, and promises of specific ordinances helps one better understand the component parts of the whole. However, it can admittedly feel somewhat mechanical and transactional, even if done in view of their associated promises. What is most essential to know and feel about the new and everlasting covenant is that it is primarily a covenant of love and belonging. It is a covenant of connectedness and deep intimacy with our Heavenly Father. President Emily Belle Freeman of the Young Women General Presidency recently alluded to this point when she said, "Perhaps you hear the words [covenant path] and think

---

112. See *Lectures on Faith* (1985), 33. "Let us here observe, that a religion that does not require the sacrifice of all things, never has power sufficient to produce the faith necessary unto life and salvation; for from the first existence of man, the faith necessary unto the enjoyment of life and salvation never could be obtained without the sacrifice of all earthly things: it was through this sacrifice, and this only, that God has ordained that men should enjoy eternal life; and it is through the medium of the sacrifice of all earthly things, that men do actually know that they are doing the things that are well pleasing in the sight of God."

CHAPTER 6: THE COVENANT RELATIONSHIP

of checkboxes. Maybe all you see is a path of requirements. A closer look reveals something more compelling. A covenant is not only about a contract, although that is important. It's about a relationship. President Russell M. Nelson taught, 'The covenant path is all about our relationship with God.'"[113]

CHAPTER SUMMARY

1. Our covenant relationship with our Father is designed to transform us into new creatures.

   a. Covenants and ordinances facilitate a process of rebirth.
   b. Covenants and ordinances create a union with God.

2. Bilateral and Unilateral Covenants

   a. We grow by making and keeping a succession of covenants with God.
   b. The gospel of Jesus Christ has both unilateral and bilateral covenants.
   c. The "covenant path" is a term referring to all covenants required for exaltation. All such covenants are bilateral, requiring action from both parties—us and God.

3. Covenantal conditions describe how to fulfill the covenant.

   a. Conditions are a standard to draw nearer to God.
   b. Conditions prepare our body and soul to enter God's presence.

4. Covenantal obligations define what we are to do to fulfill covenant conditions.

   a. Obligations are received by both parties within a covenant.
   b. Obligations provide assurance, motivation, and responsibility to recipients.

---

113. Emily Belle Freeman, "Walking in Covenant Relationship with Christ," *Liahona*, Nov. 2023, 78. See also Russell M. Nelson, "The Everlasting Covenant," *Liahona*, Oct. 2022.

The New and Everlasting Covenant

    c. God deeply wants us to understand our obligations in the covenant.

    d. Fulfilling covenantal obligations gives us access to God's power, or priesthood power.

5. Covenantal ordinances are essential to reviewing covenantal promises.

    a. All must receive covenantal ordinances to receive associated promises.

    b. Ordinances are the channels to receive covenantal promises.

    c. Ordinances must be performed and received in the manner revealed by the Lord.

Reflection Questions

- What aspects of the new and everlasting covenant stood out to you in this chapter?
- How do covenants and ordinances transform us into new creatures?
- What are the differences between unilateral and bilateral covenants of the gospel of Jesus Christ?
- What are the conditions of the covenants you have made with your Heavenly Father?
- How have you changed as you fulfill your covenant obligations? What blessings have you received as a result?
- Who do you know who would benefit from what you have learned?

7

The Covenant of Love

I attended a session of stake conference recently, and the visiting General Authority shared an experience he had with President Boyd K. Packer shortly before President Packer died. He said that the two of them were on assignment at a stake conference, and President Packer shared two experiences that had a profound effect on him. The first story referred to a time he was called out of a church meeting to come to the scene of a car crash where his teenage son and vehicle were involved. Upon arriving at the scene, President Packer was approached by a policeman who asked if he was the father of the boy driving the car. President Packer replied that he was. The policeman said that usually after a crash occurs, the last thing a teenage driver wants to do is speak to their father. But in this case, the first and only thing the boy had said to the policeman was "I need to speak with my father." After relating this story, President Packer looked at the congregation and said, "This is all that I know," then proceeded to tell the second story.

In the second story, President Packer was the visiting authority at a stake in a foreign country. Upon his arrival, he was greeted by a member of the stake presidency and taken to a member's home to spend the night. Very tired from the long day of travel, President Packer went to bed. After a few minutes in bed, he heard small footsteps approach

109

the door, enter the room, and get into bed next to him. It was a young boy, the son of the member. The room was dark, but the young boy felt through the dark and found President Packer's face and felt it for a few moments, then said, "You're not my dad. Does my dad know you're here?" President Packer replied, "Yes, your dad said I could stay here." The little boy rolled over and went to sleep. President Packer looked again at the congregation and said, "This is all that I know," and returned to his seat on the stand.

What was it that President Packer knew? I suppose many lessons could be drawn from these two stories, but a few things lie at the heart of the new and everlasting covenant. First, our Father loves us. In our moments of need, our deepest nature is to turn to Him. Why? Because we can trust Him. We can believe His word and commitments to us. His word can provide assurance to sleep soundly, even amidst our strange surroundings in a fallen world. Everything about the new and everlasting covenant is so designed to draw us nearer to God, to learn of Him, and to forge a most intimate relationship with Him. After all, He knows all about us. The challenge is for us to learn more about Him.

As it was in the Creation, when our Father commanded chaos to organize and "watched those things [He] had ordered until they obeyed" (Abraham 4:18), so it is today with us. God's love for us ensures that our agency to choose is upheld, and He made "ample provision" to ensure that all may know of His covenant and obey it in their own time. Therefore, our Father has provided that all men and women—people everywhere from all nations, kindreds, tongues, and people—will know of His covenant offering. He has left nothing to chance, and no one has been overlooked or forgotten. Of this reality we can be certain: We can trust our Father in Heaven completely.

Demographers estimate that approximately 117 billion people have lived on earth.[114] Accounting for the agency and free choice for this many of His spirit children seems daunting to us. Yet it is precisely how God has arranged things. Such a mass of "choosing" has led to large periods of time when apostasy and rebellion against God

---

114. "How Many People Have Ever Lived on Earth?," PRB, Nov. 15, 2022, https://www.prb.org/articles/how-many-people-have-ever-lived-on-earth/.

and His covenant reigned. Anciently, God scattered Israel because of their unrighteous choices, but He promised to gather them again. In our day, when men and women leave the covenant path for reasons of disobedience and rebellion, they too are left with the promise that they will be gathered together again because of God's love for them, reflecting His obligation in His bilateral covenant with all of us to help us and lead us along. Thus, we must not let our fears or worries lead us to conclude that all is lost. The Lord of the vineyard—even the Father of us all—has been at the work of arranging and gathering for a long time and has the ways and means to bring forth fruit in the most bitter spots of hardened ground.

Israel has always been a people who covenant with God to obey His laws. In the latter days, those who are willing to covenant with God in the new and everlasting covenant also covenant to gather others into the same covenantal relationship. This is done on both sides of the veil by covenant keepers through living and sharing the gospel of Jesus Christ and through vicarious ordinance work for the dead who are hearing the same gospel shared with them in the world of spirits. The work of gathering en masse begins with temples.

Within temples, the covenant is taught holistically—from before Creation through the winding-up scene. It is where the new and everlasting covenant is administered and comprehended in its fulness.[115] "What was the object of gathering the . . . people of God in any age of the world?" asked the Prophet Joseph. "The main object was to build unto the Lord a house whereby He could reveal unto His people the ordinances of His house and the glories of His kingdom, and teach the people the way of salvation; for there are certain ordinances and principles that, when they are taught and practiced, must be done in a place or house built for that purpose."[116] Our Father has arranged for His best lessons to be shared in totality in His house, away from the world, to prepare His saints to pay it forward to their spirit brothers and sisters.

---

115. "*Everything* we believe and *every* promise God has made to His covenant people come together in the temple." Russell M. Nelson, "The Temple and Your Spiritual Foundation," *Ensign* or *Liahona*, Nov. 2021, 94.

116. *The Joseph Smith Papers, Documents, Vol. 12: March 1843–July 1843*, 385.

Our Father has ensured that His covenant offering will be accelerated in the dispensation of the fulness of times. The dispensation of the fulness of times is a designated period in the history of the earth when He will "gather together in one all things in Christ, both which are in heaven, and which are on earth" (Ephesians 1:10). The priesthood authority and keys necessary to perform the various labors of the gathering have been restored to the earth (see Doctrine and Covenants 110) and are held jointly by members of the First Presidency and Quorum of the Twelve Apostles (see Doctrine and Covenants 112:30–32). The ordinance work administered within holy temples of the Lord is the epicenter of accelerating the covenant offering.

THE HOUSE OF ISRAEL

The accelerants of the covenant offering to all of God's children are a relatively select group of our Father's spirit sons and daughters called "Israel."[117] Scientists tell us that the human genome consists of 3.2 billion nucleotides, 23,500 genes, and 180,000 protein-coding regions called exons. The various combinations of these elements are what constitute unique human beings. The number of combinations of nucleotides, genes, and exons is a number so large that we cannot fathom it—almost, as it were, "as innumerable as the stars; or, if ye were to count the sand upon the seashore ye could not number them" (Doctrine and Covenants 132:31). In other words, the probability that you were even born on this earth is very, very small given the total potential humans that could have existed on this earth. What does this mean in regard to members of the house of Israel? In relative terms, to encounter one is extremely rare, and to be a member is priceless.

The new and everlasting covenant makes men and women members of the house of Israel, meaning they become an heir of the inheritance God promises to Israel. By receiving the same covenant our Father made with Abraham, Issac, and Jacob, one becomes the seed of

---

117. "In *every* age, the temple has underscored the precious truth that those who make covenants with God and keep them are children of the covenant." Russell M. Nelson, "The Temple and Your Spiritual Foundation," 94.

Abraham, Issac, and Jacob (Israel) and heirs to the same promises.[118] Those people who are not natural heirs by birth can be grafted into the family of Israel, but certain conditions must be first met. One must, first, come to the knowledge of the promises of God to Israel; second, enter into a covenant relationship with God, offered through the gospel of Jesus Christ; third, come to the knowledge of the covenant promises; and fourth, come to the knowledge of the Redeemer "that they may know how to come unto him and be saved" (1 Nephi 15:14).

Knowing of the new and everlasting covenant of our Father and the gospel in its fulness does not make a person better than anyone else, but it does obligate them to share what they know so all may be benefited thereby. Joseph Smith taught, "Souls are as precious in the sight of God as they ever were; and the Elders were never called to drive any down to hell, but to persuade and invite all men everywhere to repent, that they may become the heirs of salvation. It is the acceptable year of the Lord: liberate the captives that they may sing hosanna (see Isaiah 61:1–2)."[119] Members of the house of Israel—those who have received the new and everlasting covenant—are "the salt of the earth, and the savor of men" (Doctrine and Covenants 101:39). They assume the obligation to act as "saviors of men," an obligation they fulfill as they share the gospel of Jesus Christ and bring others into the covenant path "that they may know they are not cast off forever" (title page of the Book of Mormon). In this way, they help fulfill the Father's covenant to all of His spirit sons and daughters, furthering Jesus's "preparations" (Doctrine and Covenants 19:19) for all of us and enabling Him to act as both "the author and finisher of our faith" (Hebrews 12:2).

Our Father has neither forgotten nor left any of His children desolate. He has provided that His covenant can be extended to the living and to those who have died without knowledge of it. "The commitment to aid one another across the veil can be classified as a covenant

---

118. "In the house of the Lord, we can make the same covenants with God that Abraham, Isaac, and Jacob made. And we can receive the same blessings!" Russell M. Nelson, "The Temple and Your Spiritual Foundation," 94.

119. *The Joseph Smith Papers, Documents, Volume 4: April 1834–September 1835,* 330.

promise, part of the new and everlasting covenant," explains Elder Christofferson.[120]

One of the grandest concepts in the gospel of Jesus Christ is the concept that men can and should be more than passive observers in the cause of saving souls. In fact, each of us is obligated to become an active agent in bringing others to the covenant, an obligation we reassume in mortality on account of the agreement made before we came to earth. Elder John A. Widtsoe of the Quorum of the Twelve Apostles taught, "In our preexistent state . . . we made a certain agreement with the Almighty. . . . We agreed . . . to be not only saviors for ourselves but measurably, saviors for the whole human family. We went into a partnership with the Lord. The working out of the plan became then not merely the Father's work, and the Savior's work, but also our work."[121] Hence, "the greatest responsibility in this world that God has laid upon us is to seek after our dead."[122]

Fortunately, our Father has ensured that this can be done easily—it's as simple as helping others learn of and receive the covenant. "*Anytime* you do *anything* that helps *anyone*—on either side of the veil—take a step toward making covenants with God and receiving their essential baptismal and temple ordinances, you are helping to gather Israel," President Russell M Nelson said. "It is as simple as that."[123] Our Father has made "ample provision," and we can trust His plan completely!

There is a risk, however, to those called to act as saviors of men. It is the risk of contamination. Our obligation to bring others into the covenant does not expire, nor does it contain any quotas to fulfill. It is an everlasting obligation to all those under the covenant. The only way the obligation is removed—once assumed, that is—is by filling our lives with diversions that corrupt our desires and turn us away from our Father. The great challenge facing all under covenant is to

---

120. D. Todd Christofferson, "Sealing Power," *Liahona*, Nov. 2023, 21.

121. John A. Widtsoe, *Utah Genealogical and Historical Magazine*, Oct. 1934, 189.

122. *The Joseph Smith Papers, Documents, Volume 14: 1 January–15 May 1844,* 349.

123. Russell M. Nelson and Wendy W. Nelson, "Hope of Israel" (worldwide youth devotional, June 3, 2018), Gospel Library.

CHAPTER 7: THE COVENANT OF LOVE

act consistent with our sacred trust and maintain God's power as we do so and not go chasing after strange gods that would corrupt and consume the soul. After all, "ye cannot serve God and mammon" (see Matthew 6:24; Luke 16:13; 3 Nephi 13:24). Elder Carlos Asay described our challenge this way: "A world-renowned chemist told me that salt will not lose its savor with age. Savor is lost through mixture and contamination. Similarly, priesthood power does not dissipate with age; it, too, is lost through mixture and contamination."[124]

THE SPIRIT OF ELIJAH

One way the Father has attended to His plan in detail is through the ministry of Elijah. Elijah comes to restore the power to make the renewal of the covenant in mortality binding in heaven. His ministry is of such importance to the plan of salvation that it is mentioned in the first and last sections—as essential bookends—of the Doctrine and Covenants chronologically (see Doctrine and Covenants 2; 138:46–48). Elijah comes to turn hearts, which is much more difficult than just changing minds. To have one's heart turned, a person must come to sense the covenants, obligations, and promises of the Father's covenant, and that is precisely what Elijah came to do: "plant in the hearts of the children the promises made to the father" (Joseph Smith—History 1:39). What promises? The promises of the new and everlasting covenant. Because of His abiding love for us, our Father wants us to remember and always retain in remembrance His promises to us. "How shall God come to the rescue of this generation?" asked the Prophet Joseph. "He will send Elijah the Prophet . . [who] shall reveal the covenants to seal the hearts of the fathers to the children, and the children to the fathers. The anointing and sealing are to be called, elected, and made sure."[125] The covenants are meant to seal our

---

124. Carlos E. Asay, "Salt of the Earth: Savor of Men and Saviors of Men," *Ensign*, May 1980, 42.

125. *The Joseph Smith Papers, Documents, Volume 13: August–December 1843*, 75. Joseph also taught that "the spirit, power, and calling of Elijah is that ye have power to hold the key of the revelations, ordinances, oracles, powers and endowments of the Fullness of the Melchizedek Priesthood and of the Kingdom of God on the earth; and to receive, obtain, and perform all of the ordinances belonging to the Kingdom of God, even unto the turning

hearts to our families—past and present—and to God our Heavenly Father.

Elijah was sent to bridge a gap between us and our Father. The gap was created over long periods of time as His spirit children gave their hearts and minds to someone or something other than Him. As a result, the covenant relationship between God and mankind has been torn asunder. However, despite the collective neglect of our forefathers, our Father longs for reconnection with us. He, unlike His spirit sons and daughters generally, has not forgotten His commitment to our growth and development. His desire to connect with us remains powerful, so much so that He ensured the covenant itself possessed magnetism to draw us to Him, provided we could hear it. He wants us linked together, even by a weld (see Doctrine and Covenants 128:18).[126] So He sends Elijah to initiate our coming together, the reuniting of our hearts and minds through renewed commitment toward God. It is through Elijah's ministry that the total benefits of Jesus's "at-one-ment" can take effect. Elijah, meaning "Jehovah is my God," is sent precisely to entice us to cease "halting between two opinions" (1 Kings 18:21) and declare once and for all what His name signifies.

The Sealing Power

The sealing power restored by Elijah ensures that all acts performed in the manner and by the authority that God outlined before the foundation of the world have efficacy in heaven after men are

---

of the hearts of the fathers unto the children, and the hearts of the children unto the fathers, even those who are in heaven. This is the spirit of Elijah, that we redeem our dead, and connect ourselves with our fathers which are in heaven and seal up our dead to come forth in the first resurrection; and here we want the power of Elijah to seal those who dwell on earth to those who dwell in heaven. This is the power of Elijah and the keys and Kingdom of Jehovah." *The Joseph Smith Papers, Documents, Volume 14: 1 January–15 May 1844*, 259.

126. A weld joins together two separate pieces of metal, uniting them through heat, pressing, and hammering to combine them into a harmonious and effective whole.

CHAPTER 7: THE COVENANT OF LOVE

dead.[127] The sealing power is the ratification of all righteous acts done in the name of God for the salvation of man. Elijah's mission, power, and spirit is to unite—in every conceivable way that man and woman can be united—everyone who actively and submissively invites the Atonement of Christ into their lives. The sealing power will ultimately honor all actions, thoughts, feelings, and desires adopted by a person as they fulfill their covenantal obligations (see Doctrine and Covenants 132:7).[128] It is in this way that "everything that is good" will be restored unto us again at the Day of Judgment, and it is because of this that the righteous will abide the day of Christ's Second Coming.

Malachi tells us that if not for Elijah—the "messenger of the covenant" (Malachi 3:1)—and the sealing power, the earth would be "utterly wasted" (Doctrine and Covenants 2:3). Why? Because according to the new and everlasting covenant, the earth was created as an inheritance for covenant keepers. Its destiny was to become the celestial kingdom—to fill the measure of its creation and to be inhabited by people who have received and honored the same covenant and filled the measure of their creation. The new and everlasting covenant reunites and restores order to the human family, even the same order enjoyed prior to coming to this earth. Thus, the purpose of the sealing power is to weld us together into an eternal chain—and it is in the temple, the great symbol where heaven and earth meet, that these links are made sure and Elijah's power is manifest.

Our Father's covenant ensures no one will be forgotten. Our Father happily grants unto men and women of the covenant in mortality the ability to know those who have died and to find the names of those who are lost to us. They are all known to Him. President

---

127. "The power to validate all priesthood ordinances and make them binding both on earth and in heaven—the sealing power—is crucial for gathering and preparing a covenant people on both sides of the veil." D. Todd Christofferson, "The Sealing Power," *Liahona*, Nov. 2023, 19.

128. Elder Neal A. Maxwell, in an interview with Hugh Hewitt, was asked about family members on earth who go to different kingdoms of glory in the Resurrection and whether they would know them as family members. Elder Maxwell surmised that they would probably recognize each other but would not enjoy the familial pull enjoyed today. That "pull" or feeling of love is a gift—a gift that will have an end unless it receives the seal!

Packer explained, "Revelation comes to individual members as they are led to discover their family records in ways that are miraculous indeed. And there is a feeling of inspiration attending this work that can be found in no other. When we have done all that we can do, we shall be given the rest. The way will be opened to us."[129] President Nelson has also reminded us that the sealing power applies also to those who have gone astray. Our Father has accounted for their choices and will feel after them in His own time and in His own way.[130]

One caveat within the covenant is the condition that we do all that the Lord commands us (see Abraham 3:25), which suggests some specialized commandments to the individual to account for their unique circumstances and choices. For example, speaking to Joseph Smith, the Lord declared, "Let no one, therefore, set on my servant Joseph; for I will justify him; for he shall do the sacrifice which I require at his hands for his transgressions, saith the Lord your God" (Doctrine and Covenants 132:60). Apparently, Joseph had some transgressions that would require a special offering to the Lord. Some of us too may be called upon to experience some fiery trials as a consequence of our choices under the covenant, and like Joseph, we should likewise not "think it some[thing] strange" (Peter 4:12).

In the plan of the great God, all those under covenant in the new and everlasting covenant—with the exception of the sons of perdition—will be justified. How? Apparently, the Lord will deliver customized opportunities to serve, obey, and endure to all persons with whom He covenants, such that all of the words they offered in His name with righteous intent will be fulfilled by Him. And for any words or actions that did not measure up to the mark, God will require the necessary actions and provide adequate experiences for their sins to be forgiven, proving that He is "a perfectly just God and a merciful God also" (Alma 42:15).

Another purpose of the sealing power is to ensure that all the children of God are united together in feeling and concern for one another. The sealing power forges a connection between dispensations through time and throughout all eternity. However, one thing we

---

129. Boyd K. Packer, *The Holy Temple* (Salt Lake City, UT: Bookcraft, 1981), 20.

130. See Russell M. Nelson, "The Everlasting Covenant," *Liahona*, Oct. 2022.

learn about the sealing power is that it's only received through unity of feeling with God and when contention is eliminated from our lives. The covenants are of no efficacy without a seal, and the seal can only come upon principles of righteousness. Therefore, taught Jesus to the Nephites, "whosoever hath the spirit of contention is not of me, but of the devil, who is the father of contention and stirreth up the hearts of men to contend with anger, one with another. Behold, this is not my doctrine, to stir up the hearts of men with anger, one against another; but this is my doctrine, that such things should be done away" (3 Nephi 11:29–30).

The covenants can invite intimacy and concern for others, specifically our families, if we strive to eliminate contention from our relationships. The covenant invites connectedness socially, emotionally, physically, and spiritually if we emulate righteousness and persuade our children to do the same in their relationships. The "whole and complete and perfect union" described by Joseph occurs when men and women receive the fulness of priesthood ordinances; sacrifice their hearts, spirits, and minds to the requirements of Jesus's gospel; and strive to endure valiantly to the end of their lives. When such covenants are lived fully, then the sealing power becomes operative, and our hearts unite with those with whom we live and serve. Our hearts are filled with love for those who came before us, and our lives are devoted to serving those who will come after us.

The sealing power gathers us physically. When men and women receive the covenant of baptism, they are physically gathered into a stake and ward where they associate with like-minded people who practice living the gospel together. This association builds connection. Additionally, the covenants gather our minds by centering our thoughts upon the Savior's example and His gospel. We are challenged "to always remember" (Moroni 4:3) God and to "look unto [Him] in every thought" (Doctrine and Covenants 6:36). We strive to obtain "the mind of Christ" (1 Corinthians 2:16).

Simply put, the covenants change how we feel toward others, both the living and the dead. As we keep our covenants, our hearts are changed from stony hearts to fleshy tables upon which the Lord can place His word, forgive our sins, and fill us with His Spirit. "And the remission of sins bringeth meekness, and lowliness of heart; and because of meekness and lowliness of heart cometh the visitation of the Holy Ghost, which Comforter filleth with hope and perfect love, which love endureth by diligence unto prayer, until the end shall come, when all the saints shall dwell with God" (Moroni 8:26).

Dwelling with the Saints—fellow travelers within the covenant—and with God is the ultimate connection. The lessons that come while learning and serving in The Church of Jesus Christ of Latter-day Saints are not accidental, nor can they be dismissed as unnecessary. They are vital to our development within the covenant.

The sealing power also ratifies connections across God's grand plan that we cannot see nor fully yet appreciate. Within the new and everlasting covenant, much of what we learn is through observing what I call the ripples of our lives: "Ripples are one way we know something has happened despite our inability to see what caused it, and they help give life meaning and purpose."[131] Without an understanding of the promises of the unilateral and bilateral agreements of the new and everlasting covenant, we are liable to make attribution errors and misinterpret events around us. For example, one unilateral contract is the commitment to live the law of tithing. All who obey this law are promised an opening of "the windows of heaven" and to be blessed with blessings such "that there shall not be room enough to receive [them]." Additionally, they are promised by the Lord that "the devourer" will be rebuked and "not destroy the fruits of your ground; neither shall your vine cast her fruit before the time in the field" (Malachi 3:10–11).

The blessings here are not specifically named. Instead, what is promised is a plethora of blessings—too diverse and abundant to name—and divine timing in our lives to sustain us come what may. Consider for a moment someone who has obeyed this law. Is it possible to count the many blessings that have continually flowed into their lives? So many of our material blessings go unnoticed or are possibly misattributed by us to other influences. As human beings, we tend to attribute many fortunate outcomes in our lives to our own knowledge, actions, or intentions when, in fact, they are ripples from the interventions of our Heavenly Father on our behalf.

---

131. Joshua Savage, *Our Divine Identity* (Springville, UT: Cedar Fort, 2024), 65.

Bilateral covenants create ripples in time and eternity. Consider the impact of the actions of a woman who hears the gospel, repents of her sins, and is baptized. Her life changes as she obeys the commandments and begins to serve those around her. In time, she meets a man and receives a succession of bilateral covenants in the temple, including the final covenant of temple marriage. She and her husband cleave to each other, striving to elevate one another as they keep the commandments and counsel with the Lord in all of their doings. She bears and rears children and teaches them "to understand the doctrine of repentance and baptism by immersion" so that they too can enter the covenant path. Time passes and the process is repeated over and over again among her posterity. This woman leaves a trace of ripples in mortality through several generations. Her actions are known, but the effects of them spread out after her in ways she cannot fully fathom. So too are her works for the dead.

In the temple, we create ripples in the spirit world that we cannot see but sometimes get to feel. Within the new and everlasting covenant, ripples exist in places that we cannot see but are a result of our actions in mortality, bringing to life the Lord's promise that "if your joy will be great with one soul that you have brought unto me into the kingdom of my Father, how great will be your joy if you should bring many souls unto me!" (Doctrine and Covenants 18:16). The Lord is trying to get us to acknowledge the implications—ripples—of actions taken here on behalf others. This is something of which He knows a great deal.

The ultimate effect of all our ripples will be known in the Resurrection. There, when the book of life is opened, we will see not only our actions, our thoughts, and our words but also their effect on those around us. This sobering event will cause us much pain and sorrow if our lives have not come to resemble our righteous aspirations. At that day, all of us will be grateful for our remarkable Savior who blots out our iniquities, mistakes, shortsightedness, and indiscretions according to our repentance and faith in Him. So too, at that future day, will we acknowledge—perhaps for the first time—all that He comprehended and orchestrated on our behalf before the foundations of the earth were laid. When we see then the ripples we have left—and the stirrings those small waves have had wafting men and women everywhere toward righteousness—our hearts will expand with joy, hollowing out new space within our souls to receive "all that the Father hath," and yet still, "there will not be room enough to receive it."

HESED: A LOVING RELATIONSHIP

The new and everlasting covenant also gives us access to godly power through access to His loving influence called *hesed*. Often translated into English as "loving-kindness," hesed is "a special type of love that God has for those who covenant with Him in the new and everlasting covenant."[132] Because of the bilateral nature of the covenant between God and us in the new and everlasting covenant, each party assumes mutual obligations toward one another that are not in place outside of the covenant. We consecrate our whole self to God. We covenant to love Him above all else, to serve Him first, to obey Him, to honor Him, and to sacrifice our time, talents, and energy in building His kingdom and doing His will. He assumes an obligation—a personal obligation—to comfort us, not abandon us, lift us, guide us, strengthen us, help us, and succor us in times of need. His love, or hesed, binds Him to us in the new and everlasting covenant.

Hesed is not an ordinance but rather a loving power that obligates our Father toward us for every bilateral agreement within the new and everlasting covenant. Similarly, we should reciprocate such loving concern toward Him in our covenant agreements. This is what we strive for and what He longs for. A summary of God's and our obligations toward each other by virtue of hesed is found in Table 5.

Hesed is "a special kind of love and mercy"[133] that is not available to a person outside the covenant relationship. Hesed reflects a deep commitment by which both parties are bound to be loyal and faithful to each other. A celestial marriage is an opportunity to create this type of loving relationship with another person. A husband and wife make a covenant with God and with each other to be loyal and faithful to each other.

---

132. Russell M. Nelson, "The Everlasting Covenant."

133. Russell M. Nelson, "The Everlasting Covenant."

God's Hesed Obligations to Us[134]	Our Hesed Obligations to God
• Comfort us	• Obey His commandments
• Not abandon us	• Have no other gods before Him
• Lift us	• Sacrifice a broken heart, repeatedly
• Guide us	• Offer a contrite spirit, repeatedly
• Strengthen us	• Consecrate our whole souls to Him
• Help us	• Give our best efforts
• Succor us	

Table 5: Obligations of Hesed: Our Father's and Our Own

When God commanded the children of Israel to "have no other gods before him," he explained it was because He was "a jealous God" (Exodus 20:3–5). The word translated as jealous (*qannah*) means in Hebrew "possessing sensitive and deep feelings." God is trying to explain to Israel—and to us—that when He covenants with us, He is giving a part of Himself, a very sensitive part of Himself, to the relationship. He will not violate His commitment to us, and He pleads with us to do likewise. When we do violate our covenant with Him, He is devastated, yet His promise to us is that He will not abandon us and that His patience toward us will never cease.

What is needed for us to fulfill our hesed obligations to God? Among other things, we must come to acknowledge, understand, and commit to fulfilling the conditions of our covenants. Elder Renlund explains, "A covenant is a pledge that we should prepare for, clearly understand, and absolutely honor. Making a covenant with God is different than casually making a promise. . . . A feeble promise does not have the connecting strength to lift us above the pull of the natural flow. We make a covenant only when we intend to commit ourselves quite exceptionally to fulfilling it. We become covenant children of God and inheritors of His kingdom, especially when we identify ourselves completely with the covenant."[135] In order to enjoy the advantages of hesed, we must assume greater responsibility for

---

134. See Russell M. Nelson, "The Everlasting Covenant."

135. Dale G. Renlund, "Accessing God's Power through Covenants," *Liahona*, May 2023, 35–36.

performing our covenantal obligations to the point that they consume us, define us, and influence our identity as children of God—children of a King.

Understanding the function of hesed invites further consideration of the Savior as a model within the scriptures that illustrates the Father's hesed in action. As it turns out, through the person of His Only Begotten Son, the Father has shown us hesed in action so that we might better feel and cultivate it in our relationship with Him. As we shall see, through the life of Jesus Christ, we learn how to fulfill our obligations within a hesed relationship and how the Father fulfills His.

Chapter Summary

1. The new and everlasting covenant is a covenant of love.

    a. God has left nothing to chance when it comes to us.
    b. God will gather all of His children.
    c. God's work of gathering begins in His temple.

2. The house of Israel facilitates God's purposes of gathering.

    a. Membership in the house of Israel is a rare and priceless privilege to act in God's work.
    b. Receiving the new and everlasting covenant grants status within the house of Israel.
    c. Members of the house of Israel have covenantal obligations to gather our Father's children on both sides of the veil.
    d. The only delay in gathering is when we, as salt, become contaminated and lose our savor.

3. The spirit of Elijah is essential in the gathering of Israel.

    a. The spirit of Elijah turns hearts toward the covenant.
    b. Our Father sent Elijah to draw our hearts toward our covenantal obligations with God.

4. The sealing power binds our hearts to God eternally, uniting us with Him.

CHAPTER 7: THE COVENANT OF LOVE

    a. The sealing power unites the spirit children of God to each other, gathering us spiritually.

    b. The sealing power gathers us physically.

    c. The sealing power ratifies connections across time that we cannot see.

5. Hesed is our Father's loving influence for all of us.

    a. Hesed obligates our Father to act on our behalf.

    b. Hesed exists only within the covenant relationship.

    c. We must understand our covenant obligations to reciprocate hesed toward God.

REFLECTION QUESTIONS

- What aspects of the new and everlasting covenant stood out to you in this chapter?
- How can you show faith in the idea that our Father has left nothing to chance in His plan for us?
- How does one become a member of the house of Israel?
- How does your membership in the house of Israel motivate your actions?
- Why is Elijah's mission, and his spirit, so vital to the gathering of Israel?
- What feelings do you have for your Father as you contemplate His hesed for you?
- Who do you know who would benefit from what you have learned?

8

Jesus Christ: The Token of Our Father's Love

As discussed in chapter 5, after Adam and Eve were driven from the Garden of Eden, Heavenly Father disappeared from view behind the personage of His Only Begotten Son. From that moment forward, Jesus Christ became the front man for knowing our Father, His nature, His character, and His plan for all of us. Jesus declared, "I am the way, the truth, and the life; no man cometh unto the Father but by me" (John 14:6). Jesus became the prototype of saved beings, showing us who the Father is and how to become as He is. Additionally, and perhaps most importantly, we see how to fulfill our obligations to the Father and how He fulfills His obligations to us through the various ways He honors His Son.

Jesus Christ: The Prototype of Salvation

In *Lectures on Faith*, the Prophet Joseph testified that Jesus is the prototype of salvation, unto whose "likeness we may be assimilated."[136] He is the best and the most complete model our Heavenly Father could provide us to teach us about who He is and to demonstrate His

---

136. *Lectures on Faith* (1985), 75.

love for us in word and in deed. Jesus came to alert us to someone else who knows and loves us, to signal to us in personal and intimate ways of His loving-kindness—to remind us of a Being who has been working behind the scenes for us for a long, long time and who has bound Himself to our eternal welfare in bringing to pass the exaltation and eternal life of man.

Why must our Father work through Jesus and not directly with us? Why the need for a middleman? It is because once Adam and Eve introduced the conditions of mortality and sin, they and all of their posterity were shut out of the presence of the Father because "no unclean thing can dwell there" (Moses 6:57). Mormon described what Adam and Eve came to realize soon after they chose to fall and what it would be like for us if we were in a similar condition, now and at the Day of Judgment. He said:

> Do ye suppose that ye shall dwell with him under a consciousness of your guilt? Do ye suppose that ye could be happy to dwell with that holy Being, when your souls are racked with a consciousness of guilt that ye have ever abused his laws?
>
> Behold, I say unto you that ye would be more miserable to dwell with a holy and just God, under a consciousness of your filthiness before him, than ye would to dwell with the damned souls in hell.
>
> For behold, when ye shall be brought to see your nakedness before God, and also the glory of God, and the holiness of Jesus Christ, it will kindle a flame of unquenchable fire upon you. (Mormon 9:3–5)

When Adam and Eve fell, the first change they experienced was in their consciousness, or what they could perceive, when they discovered their nakedness before God. It is the consciousness, or awareness, of our differing natures that makes us shrink before God our Father. Our sins darken our minds and hearts, even our very souls, and the light and glory of God not only expose such darkness but also heighten our awareness of it.

Mercifully, our Father took necessary precautions to create physical distance between us and Him to make the necessary preparations to return to His presence. Jesus is the way to prepare us for the return. He is the door through which we enter the path (see John 10:7, 9), the

CHAPTER 8: JESUS CHRIST: THE TOKEN OF OUR FATHER'S LOVE

path we must walk (see John 14:6), the bread of life to sustain us (see John 6:35), the water of life to give us life (see Alma 5:34), the keeper of the gate to the Father's presence (see 2 Nephi 9:41), and the very veil we must penetrate (Hebrews 10:20) to enter again into the presence of our heavenly parents. Thus, we are commanded in all things by the Father to "hear Him" (Joseph Smith—History 1:17).

Jesus is our veil because it is only by putting on His character and attributes that we can enter the Father's presence. There is no other way. Putting on the character and attributes of Jesus is how we fulfill our part of the hesed relationship with our Father in Heaven.[137] Fully wearing well the mantle of our hesed relationship, which Jesus modeled for us, requires us to conform to four vital principles, as Jesus did. First, honoring our Father with exact obedience. Second, subjecting our will—meaning our desires, thoughts, and words—to the will of the Father, including His timing and expediency. Third, diligently seeking nourishment to our souls—body and spirit—from the Father. And fourth, bending our knee, as it were, and acknowledging the primacy of Jesus Christ in the Father's plan of redemption (see Appendix).

PRINCIPLE 1: HONOR THE FATHER WITH EXACT OBEDIENCE IN KEEPING HIS COMMANDMENTS

I think most Christians generally and willingly accept that Jesus was obedient. What is perhaps a bit less obvious is how *exact* His obedience was in all things. The earliest accounts of His life reveal that He was "about [His] Father's business" (Luke 2:49) as soon as the requirements of the law allowed. As He grew older and matured, He waited for his time to come and then "went about doing good" (Acts

---

137. It was Hugh Nibley who pointed out that the Semitic root of the word *atonement—kafar*—has "a relationship to Arabic kafata, meaning a close embrace, which [is] certainly related to the Egyptian *hpt*, the common ritual embrace written with the ideogram of embracing arms. *Hpt* may be cognate with the Latin *capto* and the Persian *kaftan*, a monk's robe and hood completely embracing the body." "The Atonement of Jesus Christ, Part 1," *Ensign*, July 1990. Thus, the garment given to Adam and Eve after their expulsion from the Garden of Eden would remind the wearer of a future restoration to God's presence through a divine embrace.

10:38). The questions must be asked: "How did He know what to do?" and "From whom did He learn it?"

Jesus answers these questions for us. He tells us that He only did what He saw His Father do (see John 5:19) and that He only spake the words given to Him from the Father (see John 12:49–50). Jesus's life was one where He actively and attentively sought exactly what to do and how to spend His time. He conscientiously sought what He should say and used His own discernment to decide how best to teach it (see 3 Nephi 17:2–3).

The strict devotion of Jesus to only say and do those things shown to Him by the Father included both big and small things. For instance, Jesus tells us that He laid down His life and took it up again at His Father's command (see John 10:18). This implies that the Father had a precise calculus in play for the biggest event in human history. Additionally, Jesus tells us that He spoke to His disciples all the words given Him of the Father (see John 15:15), suggesting that even in close-up conversational settings with the group or with an individual, Jesus wanted them to know precisely what the Father would have them know. This is benchmarking at its finest because we tend to often worry most about the words that we share in front of groups of people and perhaps not enough about the words spoken in our homes with our children. Both settings matter to the Father, and Jesus understood this perfectly.

Jesus was also exact in the manner of His leadership. For example, He tells us He sent His disciples into the world in the same manner as the Father sent Him (see John 20:21). Though we are undoubtedly expected to use our own talents within the kingdom of God and in our homes, we would be better served by reflecting—and not just occasionally—on the extent that our methods follow the Father's pattern as shown to Jesus. Perhaps in this lies a key for us to enjoy richer relationships with those we cherish most.

What motivated Jesus to be so precise, so exact in all of His doings and sayings? He tells us it is because He loves His Father (see John 14:31), His "Abba" or Papa (see Mark 14:36). Because of His love for His Father, Jesus finished the work assigned to Him by His Father (John 17:4), working late into the night until every detail was completed. This Jesus did, showing to us that He humbled Himself

CHAPTER 8: JESUS CHRIST: THE TOKEN OF OUR FATHER'S LOVE

before the Father by obedience to His commandments, according to the flesh (see 2 Nephi 31:7). And Jesus's concern for His Father's words didn't end after He uttered them. He wanted them—and still does want them—enjoyed by everyone everywhere. This is why Jesus, after rising from the tomb, ensured that all of the words of the Father were recorded in the Nephite records—so they would not be lost to us in the latter days (see 3 Nephi 23; 24; 26). If we are "to put on Christ" (Galatians 3:27), we must come to share His concern for exactness and honor toward His Father's works and words.

PRINCIPLE 2: SUBJECT OUR WILL TO THE WILL OF THE FATHER, INCLUDING HIS TIMING AND EXPEDIENCY

Jesus suffered the will of the Father in all things from the beginning (see 3 Nephi 11:11). This means that He has found great satisfaction in choosing to obey the Father's words and actions for a long time. Recall that "in the beginning" is the term Joseph used in the King Follett discourse to describe our situation before our spirits were presently organized. Jesus is trying to get us to understand that His commitment is absolute. He has placed the biggest bet possible on the Father's words and promises to guide His existence. To help us get where He is, Jesus breaks things down for us a bit to help us get our minds wrapped around where to start. He does this by sharing details about how He came to be here on earth and what He strives to do with His time. He says, "I came by the will of the Father, and I do his will" (Doctrine and Covenants 19:24). He tells us how He framed and prioritized the use of His time, stating, "I can of mine own self do nothing . . . because I seek not mine own will, but the will of the Father which hath sent me" (John 5:30). He also reminds us in this disclosure who it is that sent us here!

Jesus wants us to reflect on what we really want to accomplish in mortality—to honestly ask ourselves if we think we can do more with our time and make more of ourselves by following our own will and desires. Jesus knows better. This is why He desires that all things done on earth are according to His Father's will, the same as is done in heaven (see Luke 11:2). Because of what Jesus knows of heavenly things, He lets this unique perspective inform His earthly desires. He is not held captive by things that pass away.

Jesus and His Father are one (see John 10:30; 17:11), but we are told that the reason He was called the Son in mortality is because He subjected His flesh to His Father's will (see Mosiah 15:2), or to His Father's spirit, as Abinadi called it. By so doing, the Father gave Jesus power over death (see Mosiah 15:5, 7–8). Later on, the Father would also glorify the Son by granting Him power over the spirits of all men and women (see John 17:1–2), enabling the Son to not only "bring to pass the resurrection of the dead" but also "take upon him [humanity's] infirmities, that his bowels may be filled with mercy, according to the flesh, that he may know according to the flesh how to succor his people according to their infirmities" (Alma 7:12).

Subjecting His very human body and spirit to the very real pains of the flesh ensured that Jesus could ascend to the Father "and claim of the Father his rights of mercy" (Moroni 7:27), a reward that was fully earned and completely deserved. Just like us in times of required submission, Jesus desired something less painful. But unlike us, He submitted His will to the Father anyway (see Mark 14:36). Jesus, the ultimate finisher, both accomplished and finished the will of the Father (see Doctrine and Covenants 19:2).

Jesus's model of submission was in part to show us how the Father keeps His covenant promise with us as we submit like Jesus. For instance, Jesus promises us that whosoever does the will of the Father will be His brother or sister (see Matthew 12:50), entitled to all the same blessings as an heir. Additionally, as we witness our willingness to humble ourselves according to the flesh, and as we keep His commandments (see 2 Nephi 31:13), He promises to fill us with His Spirit to abide with us forever (see Doctrine and Covenants 20:77, 79; John 14:16, 26).

Jesus's life shows us that all things must happen in their set time and in a manner expedient to God's plan. In Greek, the word translated as *expedient* in the New Testament literally means "to bear together," implying that expedient things "create an advantage" or "make something better" for a person. For example, it was expedient for Jesus to minister among the Jews in ancient Israel, among the most wicked men in the world (see 2 Nephi 9:5; 10:3), and there will come a time when it is expedient for the Jews to believe in Jesus Christ as their Messiah (see 2 Nephi 25:16). "For it is expedient that

CHAPTER 8: JESUS CHRIST: THE TOKEN OF OUR FATHER'S LOVE

an atonement should be made; for according to the great plan of the Eternal God there must be an atonement made, or else all mankind must unavoidably perish" (Alma 34:9; see also Alma 42:9; Helaman 14:15–16). And after the Atonement had been made, it was expedient for Jesus to ascend to His Father for our sakes (see 3 Nephi 18:35). All of these things created an advantage for us, here and now, as well as generations past. Why? We do not know all of the reasons, but we trust in our Father's wisdom that expedient things do in fact "make something better."

Latter-day revelation uses the word *expedient* in a similar way to the New Testament usage in over 100 instances to describe our Father's purposes in dealing with us as He has. There is rarely an explanation of why things are the way they are. We are simply told that such things are not necessary for us now. What we know for sure is that "the Holy Ghost manifesteth all things which are expedient unto man" (Doctrine and Covenants 18:18) and that "if we ask for anything that is not expedient for [us]"—something contrary to the Father's will—"it shall turn unto [our] condemnation" (Doctrine and Covenants 88:65).

We know that in the second estate—which includes our mortal probation and our time in the spirit world—all people have all things expedient for them to work out their salvation (see 2 Nephi 2:27). Additionally, all of the revelations that have been given are expedient for us to know how to obtain eternal life (see 2 Nephi 3:19). Furthermore, the prophecies given by the Holy Ghost to men and women are limited to the expediency of God's infinite goodness. Whenever more information has been needed, God sends angels to communicate information He feels is expedient they should know as He has arranged (see Alma 12:28–29) and nothing more to ensure that our faith can be effectively developed.

For instance, the Book of Mormon deliberately contains fewer of Jesus's words than were revealed to the Nephites in total because the Father felt it expedient to try the faith of those who receive it (see 3 Nephi 26:8–10). Because what has been given has been carefully measured out, it is expedient that we do not seek to teach more than has been revealed (see Doctrine and Covenants 42:56–57). The Father encourages us to seek after knowledge of all sorts. But we understand that for now, answers come with necessary assurances, even though they can be somewhat limited. He has promised us that we will be given knowledge in all things as we seek them, assuming they are expedient for us to understand (see Doctrine and Covenants 88:78).

Jesus understood this last point perfectly and accepted it, even expressing gratitude to the Father for His wisdom in keeping certain information hidden from unprepared hearts before they were willing to receive it (see Matthew 11:25–26), and He reassured the Nephites that the Father has a set time to share His words with men and women everywhere (see 3 Nephi 23:4). The Father has every intention of bringing all truth together into a great whole, but "every kingdom in its hour, and in its time, and in its season, even according to the decree which God hath made" (Doctrine and Covenants 88:61).

In addition to bounding our access to certain information, the Lord also has placed us into His vineyard in areas of ground designed specifically to maximize our fruit-bearing capacities. This includes the use of our talents and the development of our patience and faith. Our faith in Christ, for example, can provide us power to do whatever is expedient God wills to be done and no more (see Moroni 7:33; 10:23). Our faith is to be used but also restrained. Similarly, our desires too must be restrained at times. Both our calls to serve and the material and spiritual blessings we receive are according to the expediency of the Lord (see Doctrine and Covenants 30:5; 44:1; 47:1; 71:1; 96:6, 8; 100:9). Thus, we should avoid the trap of comparing ourselves to the rich and famous within the Lord's kingdom. Our lot is working on us similar to their lot on them. Meanwhile, we must understand that while some are called to serve early in their lives and fulfill their duties quickly (see Doctrine and Covenants 61:7), others serve for longer, more visible stretches in order to receive the experience the Lord intends for them. In either case, our service in the kingdom is for a set and specific time period unto the glory of God (see Doctrine and Covenants 64:7; 72:2). In fact, we are told it is expedient that all things are done unto the glory of the Father (see Doctrine and Covenants 78:8; 111:3).

Not only is our individual service orchestrated with godly expediency, but so also are the macro concerns of His kingdom. In the early days of the Church's Restoration, the Lord revealed the expediency of the Church meeting together oft to worship and partake of the sacrament (see Doctrine and Covenants 20:75). In at least some situations, where we gather is directed by the expediency of the Lord to save souls (see Doctrine and Covenants 37:3; 100:4). The Saints learned early on that some of their labors—and by extension our own—in the kingdom can be halted, according to expediency of the Lord, to protect them, prepare hearts, and attend to personal needs known only to an omniscient God (see Doctrine and Covenants 37:1; 73:1, 3–4; 96:5; 99:6; 105:9–13). The Saints learned that money—the thing that so often corrupts and turns us askew—was to be used expediently according to the Lord's direction (see Doctrine and Covenants 84:103). Accepting some of these realities still challenges a fair share of Saints today, but some things are revealed to members of the Church first to understand and live and then to the world as it is expedient in the Lord (see Doctrine and Covenants 45:72). In this way, we get a "fast pass" to "become even as friends" of the Lord (Doctrine and Covenants 84:77)—which is, He tells us, also expedient for us.

PRINCIPLE 3: DILIGENTLY SEEKING NOURISHMENT TO OUR SPIRITS

"Blessed are all they," the Savior said, "who do hunger and thirst after righteousness, for they shall be filled with the Holy Ghost" (3 Nephi 12:6). Our bodies and our spirits are nourished as we pursue righteousness. By my count, there are twenty instances where Jesus provides us with specific ways to work righteousness in direct connection with the Father. Though there are many commandments within the gospel of Jesus Christ, it is these twenty that emphasize the attitudinal and behavioral few that Jesus modeled for us to reveal His Father's will and make it plain as day. Here I present these commandments as a starting point for the command of Jesus to "do the will of the Father" (Matthew 7:21) as opposed to learning or speaking it only.

We are to worship the Father in spirit and truth (see John 4:23), which means with our inward and outward parts, body and soul, exercising our individual agency within the precise sphere our Father has placed us in on behalf of those around us. Additionally, we are to hallow the Father's name (see Luke 11:2) as we do so, accepting His divine plan for us while acknowledging the gifts He has bestowed upon us to make a real difference in the lives of others.

We worship the Father most completely as we receive His testimony and receive the Son (see Joseph Smith Translation, John 6:44). Jesus is, after all, the Father's agent, sent in His name to do His will. Therefore, we should be willing and active in confessing the Son before men (see Matthew 10:32–33). Our knowledge of who Jesus is and what He has done for us should be something we hold up for others to see (see 3 Nephi 18:24). Furthermore, Jesus tells us specifically to "ask of God" as a son would ask of his father for whatsoever we stand in need of (see Joseph Smith Translation, Matthew 7:12–17), so we should ask our Father often and specifically for how best to let our light shine.

Jesus gives us many tactical commandments pleasing to our Father that nourish our souls. For instance, we are to fast discreetly (see Matthew 6:17–18), give alms in secret (see Matthew 6:4), honor our father and mother (see Matthew 15:4), and be unified in asking of the Father for what we need (see Matthew 18:19). Such prayers may be in the privacy of our closets but also should occur in our classes and quorums (see Matthew 6:6–8). We are to lay up treasures in heaven (see Matthew 6:20–24) and not despise little children (see Matthew 18:10), which means not to discount them physically or intellectually. In short, we are to treat all people, particularly "the least of these," like the kings and queens they are to become hereafter (see Matthew 25:35–40). All these commandments are specifically noted to please our Father in Heaven.

The commands that please our Father in Heaven are not limited to things we can do for those who love us. No, they include too those who want nothing to do with us. Of these, we are told that the Father wants us to forgive men their trespasses against us (see Matthew 6:14–15; 18:35), presumably the trespasses they know about and even those they are unaware of. Furthermore, we are to love our enemies—not in some distant, theoretical way, but actively "bless them that curse you, do good to them that hate you, and pray for them which despitefully use you" (Matthew 5:44). Holding up our light before men will undoubtedly invite persecution and turn some men and women into our enemies, but we are to persevere—as Jesus did—if only because

CHAPTER 8: JESUS CHRIST: THE TOKEN OF OUR FATHER'S LOVE

our Father wills it so. Doing so will undoubtedly "bear fruit," which good works also please our Father (see John 15:1–2; 3 Nephi 12:16; Doctrine and Covenants 58:27).

Nourishment to the body and spirit will require believing in commandments that may not come naturally to us and that may require "patience and faith" (Doctrine and Covenants 21:5). But accepting and believing in the words of Jesus's servants, the prophets, is also a prerequisite for earning the Father's favor (see Matthew 21:28–32; Jacob 4:5). In Hebrew, the words used for *word* and *thing* are the same, *Davar*, an unusual coincidence that suggests that words are concrete, tangible things that can be built up, torn down, and—in the case of Almighty God—endure and will not pass away. The implication is that when God speaks His words, He is building something real—He is putting something into the universe that will last forever. And when His authorized servants repeat His words, the effects "are the same." "Therefore, give heed unto my word which is quick and powerful, sharper than a two-edged sword, unto the dividing asunder of soul and spirit" (Doctrine and Covenants 1:38).

Following the words of God's servants consistently will require a special kind of humility and sacrifice from each of us, especially when the stakes are high. But we are told that offering a broken heart and contrite spirit helps us "rend the veil of unbelief" and discover for ourselves how the Father has fulfilled His covenant with each of us (see Ether 4:15). Such rending is reflective of a lifetime of striving to know the Father and receive eternal life (see John 17:3), which is, Jesus tells us, what life is all about. In the end, the Father really wants us to be perfect, meaning complete or finished—not according to someone else's standards but according to the laws He gives each of us. Be as perfect as you know how, just as Jesus and the Father do (see Matthew 5:48; 3 Nephi 12:48; 27:27).

PRINCIPLE 4: ACKNOWLEDGE THE PRIMACY OF JESUS CHRIST IN THE FATHER'S PLAN

From the beginning—our beginning—as spirit children of Heavenly Father, Jesus bore unique proximity to the Father. He was, in fact, with the Father in the beginning (see 3 Nephi 9:15), even in the bosom of the Father, implying special authority, connection, and unity with Him (see John 1:18; Doctrine and Covenants 76:13). Of necessity, our Father wills that "the life and light, spirit and power" of His plan are sent to us through Jesus Christ (Doctrine and Covenants 50:27), which the Father prescribes precisely to guide the Son's power to create and redeem His spirit children (see Doctrine and Covenants 76:42). Only the Father could make such designations, but it is, after all, His plan. Similarly, the Father relinquished His sheep—all of us—to His Only Begotten Son to redeem (see John 10:29). Jesus, then, from the earliest time of our existence as spirit children of our Heavenly Father, has been given responsibilities of trust from our Heavenly Father. God trusts the Son completely, and so must we!

Our Father is a glorified Man of Holiness (see Moses 6:57; 7:35), "full of grace and truth" (Doctrine and Covenants 93:11). The glory of the Only Begotten of the Father is also full of grace and truth (see Doctrine and Covenants 93:11), which glory Jesus models us to receive "in due time" (Doctrine and Covenants 93:19). Jesus is like unto and called the Father because He was conceived physically by His Father in Heaven (see Mosiah 15:3). He received the fulness of His Father's Spirit, a fulness that provided Him with "life in himself" (John 5:26) to fulfill His unique responsibilities.

In mortality, Jesus matured under His Father's direction and received grace for grace (see Doctrine and Covenants 93:12–14). To perform the works foreordained by His Father, Jesus received special authorization and came in His Father's name (see John 5:43). As a result, everything Jesus said carried convincing power and was eventually fulfilled by the Father (see Joseph Smith Translation, Matthew 19:26). Because Jesus always spoke the words of His Father, He was always heard by His Father (see John 11:41), and this includes the necessary instructions about when to begin His ministry, what words were needed by specific individuals and audiences, and where to minister at a collective and individual manner, one by one.

Our Father sent Jesus to be lifted up on a cross to "draw all men unto [him]" by His own power (3 Nephi 27:14). A curious phrase, admittedly—we don't know what it means for sure. One possibility is that the Father has designed His plan such that each of us has been sent to mortality and been provided with experiences necessary to be enticed to choose Jesus of our own free will. For some, such choosing

CHAPTER 8: JESUS CHRIST: THE TOKEN OF OUR FATHER'S LOVE

will occur willingly "because of the word." But for others, such humility and seeking will come only after they "have been compelled to be humble" (Alma 32:13). To help facilitate men knowing the Son, the Father glorified Jesus by giving Him power over the spirits of all men, in advance of the Atonement (see John 17:1–2). Coupled with the unique endowment of "life in himself," which the Father provided Jesus at the time of His birth, Jesus could fully apply His works to both the spirits and bodies of humanity. Jesus—and *only* Jesus—was uniquely prepared in every way to do for us what we could not do for ourselves.

The Father was always with Jesus in mortality (see John 16:32), which suggests a unique blend of seeking and submissiveness on Jesus's part. However, to make His experience perfect, the Father hid (or withheld) His immediate presence from Jesus at the time of His Atonement. We know this because of the special disclosure captured by those few witnesses who saw and heard Jesus ask why the Father had forsaken Him (see Matthew 27:46; Mark 15:34). The distance Jesus felt then had nothing to do with the Father's physical location—it was just in Jesus's perception. Fortunately for us, this space of separation ensured that Jesus's victory was completely His own and sufficient for all of us.

Through it all, Jesus became our Advocate with the Father (see Doctrine and Covenants 29:5; 32:3; 45:2), uniquely able to "claim his rights of mercy for the children of men" (Moroni 7:27). Jesus pressed forward and kept His Father's commandments and abode in His love, which is also His joy (see John 15:10). And because He did so, the Father made it absolute that you and I cannot follow Jesus without keeping the commandments the Father gave to Jesus (see 2 Nephi 31:10). No one can come unto Christ except He does the will of the Father (see Joseph Smith Translation, John 6:65), and this Jesus perfectly and completely demonstrated. Jesus honored His Father, and His atoning sacrifice became the fulcrum upon which the entire plan of salvation turns, with His name as the very foundation upon which eternal life rests.

Jesus honored His obligations with the Father in Their hesed relationship, and because He did so, the Father honors us in our relationships with Him. He favors us, here and now, by sharing His love with us because the Father loves those who love the Son (see John 16:27) and those who will have Him to be their God (see 1 Nephi 17:40). He blesses The Church of Jesus Christ by "manifesting His works in it" (3 Nephi 27:7–10). He honors His Son and us when He blesses us with His Spirit as we witness our willingness to take upon us Jesus's name and always remember Him (see 3 Nephi 18:7, 11). Additionally, He sanctifies us through Jesus's words, or the truth (see John 17:17), as we embrace it.

As we become one with Jesus and the Father, we are purified from our sins through faith and obedience to Jesus's gospel (see 3 Nephi 19:29). Such purification comes by the Father shedding forth His love (see 1 Nephi 11:22), or charity, "upon all who are true followers of his Son" (Moroni 7:48), which love purifies them and makes them the sons and daughters of God. It is because of the Father's honoring of Jesus and His own sanctification that He ensures we can be so sanctified by keeping His words (see John 17:19). Such cleansing receives the ultimate seal the Father can provide, the seal of eternal life, which seal is possible because He first sealed up the Son unto eternal life (see John 6:27). Therefore, everyone who believes on the Son shall have eternal life (see John 6:40). The promise of eternal life also carries the promise of improved proximity to the Father. Jesus tells us that whoever loves Him will be loved by the Father and will be visited by Them (see John 14:21, 23). The Father so honors the Son, such that Jesus can reveal the Father to others (see Matthew 11:27).

Even after our mortal sojourn has ended, the Father continues to honor us through the Son as part of His hesed obligation. This occurs as we share the same glory with the Son in the First Resurrection (see John 17:24). And because the Resurrection triggers our judgment "before the pleasing bar of the Great Jehovah," Jesus—"the Eternal Judge of both quick and dead" (Moroni 10:34)—will confess before the Father those who confessed Him before men in mortality (see Matthew 10:32–33). However, the Father's respect for the Son also carries heavy implications for those who reject Jesus's mission, His works, and His words. He tells us that denying His works is to also deny the Father and is a form of hate, and to hate Jesus is to hate the Father (see John 15:23–24). Anyone who finds themselves in such a situation will be condemned by the Father because they wouldn't do

CHAPTER 8: JESUS CHRIST: THE TOKEN OF OUR FATHER'S LOVE

the things Jesus commanded them to do (see 3 Nephi 18:33). Our Father's commitment to His covenant obligation to honor His Son is ultra sharp, "quick and powerful, sharper than a two-edged sword, to the dividing asunder of both joints and marrow; therefore, give heed unto my word" (Doctrine and Covenants 11:2).

Yes, anyone who serves Jesus, with an honest heart and in all diligence, will be honored by the Father (see John 12:26). Just as Jesus inherited "all that the Father hath" (John 16:15), so too are we promised to "receive all that the Father hath" (Doctrine and Covenants 84:38), and this "according to the oath and covenant of [our] Father, which he cannot break, neither can it be moved" (Doctrine and Covenants 84:42). We can trust our Father. Of this we can be sure.

CHAPTER SUMMARY

1. Jesus Christ is the prototype of salvation.

    a. Jesus became our Mediator after the Fall of Adam and Eve.
    b. Jesus is the veil between us and the Father.
    c. Four principles help us "put on" Christ and penetrate the veil.

2. Honor the Father with exact obedience.

    a. Jesus was exactly obedient in all things.
    b. Jesus was obedient in what He said.
    c. Jesus was obedient in His leadership.

3. Subject our will to the will of the Father.

    a. Jesus suffered the will of the Father in all things.
    b. Jesus let the Father's priorities guide His own.
    c. Jesus received power over the flesh and the spirit.
    d. Jesus embraced "expedient" things.

4. Diligently seek nourishment to body and spirit.

    a. Jesus revealed specific commandments to do the Father's will.
    b. Jesus revealed commandments that please the Father.

5. Acknowledge the primacy of Jesus Christ in the Father's plan.

    a. Jesus has a unique proximity to the Father.

    b. Jesus was mentored from the beginning by the Father.

    c. Jesus was given to "draw all men unto him."

    d. Jesus honored His covenantal obligations.

    e. The Father blesses us as a way to honor the Son.

REFLECTION QUESTIONS

- What aspects of Jesus's role in the new and everlasting covenant stood out to you?
- In what ways is Jesus the veil between us and the Father?
- How do the four principles outlined in the chapter help you "put on" Christ?
- How does the life of Jesus Christ motivate your actions?
- When was the last time you chose to act or say something because of Jesus Christ?
- How do you acknowledge the primacy of Jesus Christ in your life?
- Who do you know who would benefit from what you have learned?

9

THE HOLY GHOST: OUR CONSTANT COMPANION

IN JANUARY 2024, PRESIDENT JEFFREY R. HOLLAND PRESIDED OVER a regional leadership training. His remarks were short, coming on the heels of an extended hospitalization. To those in attendance, he stated, "I am basing my whole life on God's promises."[138] These profound words lie at the heart of what membership in The Church of Jesus Christ of Latter-day Saints is all about. I mean, are not all members doing as President Holland? By remaining an active participant in the Lord's Church, haven't you also chosen a path to believe in the promises of our Heavenly Father, a path tied to His covenant to us all? Whether you are yet aware of the implications of such a choice, the answer is unequivocally "Yes!" We do what we do, we endure what we endure, and we give what we give because we believe in the words of "the Most High God" and His promises to each of us.

Our Father has so equipped His plan of redemption to reward His faithful children and see them through the difficult challenges of mortality. This special provision is provided through the administration

---

138. Jeffrey R Holland, Regional Leadership Training, Jan. 19, 2024, Phoenix, AZ.

of the third member of the Godhead, even the Holy Ghost. Recall from chapter 4 that three personages entered into a covenant to see the Father's plan of salvation through to its end. The Holy Ghost is one of those three personages and fills a crucial role in ensuring that the plan of redemption is brought to pass. Why? Because each of the spirit children of our heavenly parents needs to navigate mortality without the aid of memory from our premortal state. In effect, we are driving blind. However, the Holy Ghost is sent "to bring all things to [our] remembrance" (John 14:26), which includes precious information and conviction of who we were before we came to earth. Furthermore, each of us, here in this fallen world, would struggle to discern truth from error. President Oaks explained that the Holy Ghost "can dwell in us and perform the essential role of communicator between the Father and the Son and the children of God on earth."[139] In this role, the Holy Ghost can "lead us into all truth" (John 16:13).

Additionally, the Holy Ghost helps forge and weld (seal) our relationship with our Savior and our Father in Heaven. It is His witness, which flows from our faith in Christ, that helps us know Them more fully and trust in Their promises as we act in faith and obedience to Their commandments. Finally, the Holy Ghost fulfills an essential mission in helping us become "new creatures in Christ" as we fulfill our covenant obligations. He does this by purifying us and sanctifying our hearts, changing—as it were—our very natures in fulfillment of the Father's covenant promise to us (see 2 Nephi 31:17; 3 Nephi 27:20; Moroni 6:4). The promise of the Holy Ghost is the ultimate "promise of the Father" (Acts 1:4; Doctrine and Covenants 95:9), a promise we receive by always remembering the Son and keeping His commandments and, if fulfilled, will be with each of us always (see Moroni 4:3; 5:2; Doctrine and Covenants 20:77, 79).

As children of the covenant, we have a special role to play in fulfilling the new and everlasting covenant in the last days,[140] and the Holy Ghost helps us here too. The Holy Ghost "enlighteneth every

---

139. Dallin H. Oaks, "The Godhead and the Plan of Salvation," *Ensign* or *Liahona*, May 2017, 102.

140. "While some aspects of that covenant have already been fulfilled . . . the Book of Mormon teaches that this Abrahamic covenant will be fulfilled only in these latter days! It also emphasizes that . . . ours is the privilege to participate

CHAPTER 9: THE HOLY GHOST: OUR CONSTANT COMPANION

man through the world, that hearkeneth to the voice of the Spirit. And everyone that hearkeneth to the voice of the Spirit cometh unto God, even the Father. And the Father teacheth him of the covenant which he has renewed and confirmed upon you, which is confirmed upon you for your sakes, and not for your sakes only, but for the sake of the whole world" (Doctrine and Covenants 84:46–48). The Holy Ghost guides us toward the Father—and by extension the Son—who teaches us of the covenant, which is given to save the world.

Nothing is more important for us to know today than the covenant promises of our Father of Heaven to each of us (see 1 Nephi 22:9). And for this cause, that men might be made partakers of the glories which were to be revealed, the Lord sent forth the fulness of His gospel, His everlasting covenant, "reasoning in plainness and simplicity" (Doctrine and Covenants 133:57), "that [His] everlasting covenant might be established" (Doctrine and Covenants 1:22). "Because we have the truth about the Godhead," taught President Oaks, "our relationship to Them, the purpose of life, and the nature of our eternal destiny, we have the ultimate road map and assurance for our journey through mortality. We know whom we worship and why we worship. We know who we are and what we can become (see Doctrine and Covenants 93:19). We know who makes it all possible, and we know what we must do to enjoy the ultimate blessings that come through God's plan of salvation."[141] The Holy Ghost inspires, guides, and shows us how to deliver the covenant offerings to our friends and neighbors and fulfill our Father's purposes.

The Holy Ghost also enables us to attain what the Apostle Paul described as "the measure of the stature of the fulness of Christ" (Ephesians 4:13). To develop and ultimately possess such stature individually, each of us must become far more than what we currently are. We need to learn what to do and be assisted in how best to apply what we learn. Fortunately, the Holy Ghost plays both a confirming and showing role to each of us. Nephi explained, "Angels speak by the power of the Holy Ghost; wherefore, they speak the words of Christ.

---

personally in the fulfillment of these promises." Russell M. Nelson, "The Gathering of Scattered Israel," *Ensign* or *Liahona*, Nov. 2006, 79.

141. Dallin H. Oaks, "The Godhead and the Plan of Salvation," 103.

Wherefore, I said unto you, feast upon the words of Christ; for behold, the words of Christ will tell you all things what ye should do" (2 Nephi 32:3). Additionally, he adds, "If ye will enter in by the way, and receive the Holy Ghost, it will show unto you all things what ye should do" (2 Nephi 32:5).

We first learn the words of Christ through the Holy Ghost, and then we are shown how best to live and apply them by the Holy Ghost in our daily lives. The Holy Ghost will, as Jesus promised us, "guide us into all truth" (John 16:13).

Such tactical and day-to-day support from the Holy Ghost builds our faith in the Savior and our Father's plan as we act upon His promptings. The cyclical nature of learning what to do, receiving guidance on how to do it, and having the knowledge confirmed by the Holy Ghost to our minds and hearts is a process of conversion. It is more than just a process of learning— and thankfully so. President Oaks explained that "it is not even enough for us to be *convinced* of the gospel; we must act and think so that we are *converted* by it. In contrast to the institutions of the world, which teach us to *know* something, the plan of salvation and the gospel of Jesus Christ challenge us to *become* something."[142] Our covenant responsibilities include helping God bring to pass the gathering of His elect and becoming new creatures in Christ. Obedience to the promptings of the Holy Ghost enables such a transformation.

Because each of us is an agent, the Holy Ghost will not force His influence upon us. Instead, we are commanded to "receive the Holy Ghost" (2 Nephi 31:13).[143] Elder Bednar explained that work is required, both inside and out, to fulfill the command we all are given to receive the Holy Ghost. He explained, "The Holy Ghost does not become operative in our lives merely because hands are placed upon our heads and those four important words are spoken. As we receive this ordinance, each of us accepts a sacred and ongoing responsibility

---

142. Dallin H. Oaks, "The Godhead and the Plan of Salvation," 103.

143. "These four words—'Receive the Holy Ghost'—are not a passive pronouncement; rather, they constitute a priesthood injunction—an authoritative admonition to act and not simply to be acted upon." David A. Bednar, "Receive the Holy Ghost," *Ensign* or *Liahona*, Nov. 2010, 95.

to desire, to seek, to work, and to so live that we indeed 'receive the Holy Ghost' and its attendant spiritual gifts."[144]

The companionship of the Holy Ghost is vital for us to fulfill our covenantal obligations, draw closer to our Heavenly Father, and overcome the challenges of mortality. As President Nelson has so famously warned, "In coming days, it will not be possible to survive spiritually without the guiding, directing, comforting, and constant influence of the Holy Ghost."[145]

Learning more about the methods of this special witness, then, is essential for each of us. The worry, of course, is that many carry within their own minds incorrect, or at least incomplete, ideas of how the Holy Ghost communicates with us, which may lead to feelings of inadequacy, confusion, or even rebellion against our Father's covenant. Personally, I have seen close friends leave the strait and narrow path because they could not get the answers they were seeking from God. Such answers were of course available, but in these cases, my friends carried incorrect assumptions about how to obtain answers to prayer through the Holy Ghost, how to adequately prepare themselves, and in what manner the answers might be provided. In the final chapter, we pursue answers to these questions through the experiences of one uniquely prepared to share them.

Chapter Summary

1. The Holy Ghost rewards and sustains the faithful.

    a. The Holy Ghost is a communicator between God and man.
    b. The Holy Ghost helps us fulfill our covenantal obligations.
    c. The Holy Ghost helps us become more like Jesus.
    d. The Holy Ghost helps us deal with the challenges of mortality.

---

144. David A. Bednar, "Receive the Holy Ghost," 95.

145. Russell M. Nelson, "Revelation for the Church, Revelation for Our Lives, *Ensign* or *Liahona*, May 2018, 96.

Reflection Questions

- What aspects of the Holy Ghost's role in the new and everlasting covenant stood out to you?
- In what ways is the Holy Ghost our communicator between us and the Father?
- How has the Holy Ghost helped you understand and fulfill your covenantal obligations?
- How does the Holy Ghost motivate your thoughts and behavior?
- When was the last time you chose to act or say something because of promptings from the Holy Ghost?
- When was the last time you acknowledged the Holy Ghost's influence in your life?
- Who do you know who would benefit from what you have learned?

10

LESSONS ON REVELATION

PRESIDENT HENRY B. EYRING KNOWS SOMETHING OF REVELATION. He has been uniquely tutored over a lifetime of experience. When he was a young father, he had an experience that changed his life and enhanced his ability to recognize the influence of the Holy Ghost. The experience came as he was pondering the work his father-in-law was doing on behalf of his young family. As he pondered, he recalled, "I heard in my mind—not in my own voice—these words: 'I'm not giving you these experiences for yourself. Write them down.'" President Eyring went inside the house and began to write. He said:

> I didn't go to bed. Although I was tired, I took out some paper and began to write. And as I did, I understood the message I had heard in my mind. I was supposed to record for my children to read, someday in the future, how I had seen the hand of God blessing our family. . . . And so I wrote it down, so that my children could have the memory someday when they would need it. I wrote down a few lines every day for years. I never missed a day no matter how tired I was or how early I would have to start the next day.[146]

---

146. Henry B. Eyring, "Remember, Remember," *Ensign* or *Liahona*, Nov. 2007, 66–67.

The journals and reflections of President Eyring began that day and continue—though the form has changed a bit—until this day. Just think of it: daily reflections for over fifty years. "Before I would write," recorded President Eyring, "I would ponder this question: 'Have I seen the hand of God reaching out to touch us or our children or our family today?' As I kept at it, something began to happen. . . . I became ever more certain that our Heavenly Father hears and answers prayers. . . . And I grew more confident that the Holy Ghost can bring all things to our remembrance—even things we did not notice or pay attention to when they happened."[147] The results, for us, are unique, contemporary reflections on the variety of methods used by the Holy Ghost to build faith in God and His plan for us. In this chapter, I will attempt to distill the various methods, as described by President Eyring,[148] to help each of us better fulfill our covenant obligations within the new and everlasting covenant.

President Eyring: A Case Study on Revelatory Methods of the Holy Ghost

Our transformation into new creatures occurs as we grow in our ability to seek and receive revelation from God through the Holy Ghost. Such transformation is evident in the life of President Eyring and can be the same for us too. The Holy Ghost is the messenger of the Father's covenant, leading us along (see Doctrine and Covenants 78:18) through a variety of revelatory methods to our minds and hearts. Some of the common methods experienced and captured by President Eyring are summarized in Table 6.

No one is the same in terms of their spiritual maturation or in their spiritual gifts. Therefore, we must allow one another a great deal of latitude in not only *how* we experience the promptings from the Holy Ghost but also in the *frequency* of such promptings.

---

147. Henry B. Eyring, "Remember, Remember," 67.

148. See Robert I. Eaton and Henry J. Eyring, *I Will Lead You Along: The Life of Henry B. Eyring* (Salt Lake City, UT: Deseret Book, 2013). My research on the lessons and methods of the Holy Ghost come from my own reading of President Eyring's journal entries in this volume.

CHAPTER 10: LESSONS ON REVELATION

Revelation to the Mind	Revelation to the Heart
• New thought • "Aha" experience • Remembrance • Voice in the mind • Dreams • Enlightenment around existing thoughts • Discernment • Conviction around new or existing thoughts • Stupor, forgetting, or loss of conviction around a thought or idea	• Peace and contentment • "Feels" right • Burning • Negative feelings • Warnings • Directions • Pounding of the heart or other physical sensation

Table 6: Common Revelatory Methods of the Holy Ghost to the Mind and Heart

President Eyring's experiences with family members and in counsel with Church members over his lifetime provide a type of template the Lord uses in His communications with us through the Holy Ghost. The relevant dimensions seem to be how direct He chooses to be with us and how frequently He communicates with us. Table 7 (below) attempts to illustrate the frequency and directness of such interactions. The top right quadrant of the table is the Lord's full covenantal promise of the constant companionship of the Holy Ghost. Such a blessing provides a constant flow of the Spirit of God (high frequency) and also high directness, including "the privilege of receiving the mysteries of the kingdom of heaven, to have the heavens opened unto them, to commune with the general assembly and church of the Firstborn, and to enjoy the communion and presence of God the Father, and Jesus the mediator of the new covenant" (Doctrine and Covenants 107:19).

In the other corner of the table is the lack of spiritual manifestations in both frequency and directness. This condition occurs through the hardening of one's heart, as was the case with Laman and Lemuel in the Book of Mormon. Other manifestations of the Holy Ghost, which are less frequent than "constant" and less direct than a personal manifestation, are shown. Notice that the Holy Ghost seems content

151

to work primarily in the lower right quadrant of the table, with low directness and high frequency, to build our spiritual receptivity toward His promise of constant companionship where the promise to "always have His Spirit to be with [us]" (Doctrine and Covenants 20:77) is fulfilled.

	Low	Frequency	High
High	Visitations Visions Audible voices Dreams		Constant companionship
Directness		Clear voice in mind, as if audible to the ears Still small voice to mind and heart	
Low	Past feeling Vanity and unbelief		Light of Christ

Table 7: Interaction and Directness of Spiritual Promptings

Speaking to newly called mission presidents, President Packer reinforced the idea of the low-directness bottom quadrant as the primary method the Holy Ghost uses to build our spiritual receptivity and spark spiritual growth:

> The Spirit does not get our attention by shouting or shaking us with a heavy hand. Rather it whispers. It caresses so gently that if we are preoccupied, we may not feel it at all. . . . Occasionally it will press just firmly enough for us to pay heed. But most of the time, if we do not heed the gentle feeling, the Spirit will withdraw and wait until we come seeking and listening and say in our manner and expression, like Samuel of ancient times, "Speak [Lord], for thy servant heareth." (1 Sam. 3:10.) I have learned that strong, impressive spiritual experiences do not come to us very frequently. And when they do, they are generally for our own edification, instruction, or correction.[149]

---

149. Boyd K. Packer, "The Candle of the Lord," *Ensign*, Jan. 1983.

Chapter 10: Lessons on Revelation

Revelation is best received when we have fostered the right environment within and without ourselves. For instance, we are counseled to "stand in holy places" and "with holy people,"[150] ensuring that both the company we keep and the places we frequent are conducive to spiritual visitations. We have been given certain commandments to safeguard our mental and physical fidelity, but such commandments also are "principles with a promise," which, if followed, screen our thoughts from corroding influences and protect our bodies from harmful addictions (whether big or small). Clearly, the principles of promise are meant to keep us focused on the Lord and not any of the lesser gods whose sole purpose is to satisfy our own vanity.

Internally speaking, revelation is a function of attitude as much as supplication or study.[151] We must really want to know what God wants to have done and be willing to act righteously in seeing it fulfilled. As President Eyring taught, "If you want to receive the companionship of the Holy Ghost, you must want it for the right reasons. Your purposes must be the Lord's purposes. If your motives are too selfish, you will find it difficult to receive and sense the promptings of the Spirit. The key for me and for you is to want what the Savior wants. Our motives need to be driven by the pure love of Christ. Our prayers need to be 'All I want is what you want. Thy will be done.'"[152]

Beyond the usual ways one experiences revelation from the Holy Ghost summarized in Table 7, President Eyring describes several less common methods and the settings in which such methods are likely to be used. For instance, feelings of absolute clarity, or "aha" experiences, are likely to occur when humbly listening for answers from your spouse, from presiding Church officers, or from close friends and acquaintances. Additionally, enlightenment or conviction around new or existing thoughts may not come as complete answers. Instead, they may come first as a feeling—perhaps you see something that seems out of place but you cannot identify exactly what it is—that becomes clearer over time. Gaining the clarity you seek in such instances serves as an invitation to ponder and pray for further clarity from the Lord.

---

150. See Gary E. Stevenson, "Promptings of the Spirit," *Liahona*, Nov. 2023, 45.

151. See Boyd K. Packer, "The Candle of the Lord."

152. Henry B. Eyring, "Our Constant Companion, *Liahona*, Nov. 2023, 94.

At the same time, such situations may be presented with absolute clarity to others first, which helps spur the increased clarity you are praying for. In such instances, we should be careful to not dismiss or judge incorrectly the negative feeling of unease as something not from the Holy Ghost. We must be open to learning more through the process of asking, seeking, and knocking.

Sometimes revelation comes as an assurance to abandon previous ideas—and even work—that were headed down the wrong track and to accept new ideas as they arrive in the Lord's timing. President Eyring mentioned times in his professional work as well as in his Church service when presentations and written remarks were to be set aside and he was to work without notes—something that takes great faith to do, especially for those of us who value perception over content. Working with thoughts "in the very hour, yea, in the very moment" (Doctrine and Covenants 100:6) is something that takes great trust in God to implement!

The Lord's revelations to Oliver Cowdery in Doctrine and Covenants 8 and 9 introduce the idea of communication to the mind and heart through a burning of the bosom when something you have asked for is right. According to President Eyring, this sensation in the chest is a clue to write it down. On the other hand, the feeling in the mind is a voice, but it is a voice you feel more often than you hear. Unless you have experienced this for yourself, this idea makes absolutely no sense at all. Why would you describe something you feel as a voice? It's because the feeling comes with so much clarity, at times, that your mind believes it has heard something familiar.

The voice often is accompanied by urges or nudges to do something. For example, when counseling someone with challenges, the voice can impress upon you to "keep talking" or follow a string of thoughts in your mind. It might at times prompt you to do something not according to the general rules or norms of the group you're with. It may even urge you to deliver a message to someone even while fearful of the outcome, or not deliver a message you planned to share and worked and prayed to prepare. Sometimes, while teaching or instructing, you might feel the voice to call on someone who has not raised their hand but in whose answer lies the springboard for the next round of discussion. And when called upon to serve in an assignment that you feel is beyond your current preparedness, you may feel the voice urge you to confess every unresolved sin and show gratitude for the Atonement of Jesus Christ. The voice of the Holy Ghost—the Spirit of the Lord—carries at times strong impressions to act in accordance with the Father's will.

The Holy Ghost works through visual imagery as often as He works through feelings to our minds and hearts. Dreams and memories are frequently mentioned within the standard works. Also common—but perhaps dismissed by us too quickly—are the pictures presented to our minds to solve our various problems. President Eyring frequently describes his experiences of seeing an image, or picture, with an accompanied feeling of love. Sometimes the pictures need to be pondered over and interpreted through prayer and the process of time in order to fully comprehend it. At other times, clear mental images in answer to prayer come to provide direction and guidance. Such instances are reminiscent of Nephi's experience with receiving instructions to build a ship (see 1 Nephi 17:8), Joseph Smith's knowledge of where to find the Nephite record (see Joseph Smith—History 1:42), or President Nelson's view of an unknown surgical procedure to fix a failing tricuspid valve.[153]

Sometimes the pictures the Holy Ghost provides are of specific scriptures where recorded answers from the Lord are already given. Such scriptures can be given to confirm a string of thoughts you have been receiving for the past few weeks, or the scripture might be given for you to give to someone else seeking answers. However, one must not assume that just because they're directed to a verse of scripture, they are also directed to expound upon the meaning to the individual. We need to learn to stay within our lane with sacred communication and not assume more than what the Lord intends. Scriptures can also come to mind to address problems that are seemingly unrelated to the immediate problem at hand but that contain the Lord's views on the subject. In such instances, we need extra humility to allow both our mind and our knees to bend—all the way down to the ground!

Sometimes we're blind to the dangers in front of us (see Doctrine and Covenants 10:37) or need more wisdom than we now have (see

---

153. Russell M. Nelson, "Sweet Power of Prayer," *Ensign* or *Liahona*, May 2003, 8.

Joseph Smith—History 1:12) to accomplish our desires, and the Holy Ghost helps us here too. When facing decisions where we are the final decider, the pressure can feel daunting and the fear of making a mistake is real. The Holy Ghost can, if we seek it, provide warnings prior to our need to decide. And though the decisions remain with us, the warnings test us to learn if we will hearken in advance of knowing the outcome. At times we are so certain of a course to pursue that the Holy Ghost may provide a type of "stupor of thought" (Doctrine and Covenants 9:9), which is not the same as forgetting something but will cause it to have a reduced sway over our thinking, opening us up to new possibilities. At other times, the stupor is a physical loss of words, or inability to speak, such that we are encouraged to listen more and get out of our own way.

On occasion, we may feel a rebuke, meaning absolute knowledge that what we have thought or what we have done is incorrect and must be corrected. But these feelings come only to those who love the truth more than their own ideas and are willing to repent rather than defend poor behavior.

On occasion, the Holy Ghost provides us with specific knowledge about an individual to help us know when to disagree with them. But once again, these treasures are reserved for those who will speak with pure motives and have no intention to injure. Sometimes the Holy Ghost delivers assurance to us from a loving Father in Heaven that our thoughts are His thoughts and our motives are pure, like when the words to a fully formed address are provided to us despite our lack of an immediate audience and at the same time to another who has both the opportunity and the following to deliver it. Such instances give us the assurance that we are on the right track, regardless of who delivers the words.

The Holy Ghost is such a subtle companion, one who we invite into our lives through careful scrutiny of our external and internal lives. No wonder the Prophet Joseph—who perhaps is the great model to all of us in inviting the presence of the Holy Ghost into our lives in this dispensation—taught us, "A fanciful and flowery and heated imagination beware of; because the things of God are of deep import;

CHAPTER 10: LESSONS ON REVELATION

and time, and experience, and careful and ponderous and solemn thoughts can only find them out."[154]

Revelation, in all its varieties, is intended to "ground and settle" us "[in] the hope of the gospel" (Colossians 1:23). President Eyring provides several experiences when revelation does precisely this. For instance, revelation to our mind and heart removes fear and anxiety in the face of the unknown by giving precious insight and helping us discern patterns and connections in our lives. Additionally, it blesses us to help others who struggle or are temporarily shaken by the mighty storm beating upon them (see Helaman 5:12) by first discerning and then describing the relevant feelings and yearnings of their hearts to give them knowledge of what to say or do to navigate or perhaps even endure their personal storm. Such knowledge from the Holy Ghost really is instant and is greater than any knowledge gained through our own efforts, no matter the amount of time we may have invested. In short, He is an all-knowing Comforter and Revelator who knows more than we know and stands ready to provide a special peace in the midst of uncertainty.

The Holy Ghost is also the ultimate prioritizer of information and possible solutions, giving insight that allows the "key issue" to become clear amidst a complex problem. Sometimes His presence gives insight that we should remain silent, especially when words would increase heat without the hope of persuasion. And sometimes, on occasion, the Holy Ghost gives sweet, personal assurance that our decisions bear the approval of heaven, even if they are without the approval of priesthood leaders or other well-intentioned servants of God. Such information would be given for our personal assurance and not to justify a course of action inconsistent with Church doctrine or government.

With such a variety of methods in motion, one wonders if the Holy Ghost—who delivers the revelations of the Father and Son[155]—is given the autonomy to deliver the messages according to the needs of the receiver. This might be the case. If so, His choice of methods can teach us more about who he is and what he values than we

---

154. *The Joseph Smith Papers, Documents, Volume 6: June 26–August 4, 1839*, 368.

155. See David A. Bednar, "Receive the Holy Ghost," *Ensign* or *Liahona*, Nov. 2010, 94.

have perhaps considered. Consider the fact that revelation from the Holy Ghost can be blocked when we cover ourselves with a pavilion of motivations that draw us away from God and make Him seem distant and inaccessible. Additionally, revelation is diminished through heated competition with others. What does this teach us about the Holy Ghost? For one, it shows us that His greatest desire is to be near the Father and the Son, and He will not follow us when we knowingly enter—in our minds or with our bodies—"enemy territory." Second, His preference is for unity, where contention and self-aggrandizement are eliminated. Hence, competition to place ourselves above another—and often at their own expense—is something He despises and will not sanction with His influence or presence.

Another way we learn about the Holy Ghost is through His choice of timing. Sometimes revelation comes quickly if the circumstances require it. It may or may not come at the time of the initial request, but it will come when required, teaching us that the Holy Ghost is both perfectly patient and discerning of our unique circumstances. Furthermore, not all answers to all questions will be answered at the same time; they will come line upon line as the receiver is able to receive, indicating the Holy Ghost's perfect awareness of our spiritual receptivity and susceptibility. The Holy Ghost will warn us when our minds are at rest of certain actions that need to be taken, revealing His keen sense of when we are most likely to listen and accept His subtle communications.

The Holy Ghost also trusts us and our ability to consider multiple pieces of information and come to a correct conclusion. Thus, He is often willing to let the balance of evidence indicate the Lord's will without providing accompanying personal confirmation. Instead, He waits and provides the confirmation after the decision to act is made as a witness to the truthfulness of our desires. This is because He knows that sometimes a delayed validation does more to increase our faith and trust in the Father and the Son than any express witness could. Yet revelation can and does come "in the very hour, and in the very moment" (Doctrine and Covenants 100:6) to guide us on what should be done or said, even from conversations preceding and leading up to a talk to be delivered. This is because revelation comes in proportion to the level of obligations and concern we feel while doing the Lord's work.

The Holy Ghost not only loves to honor the Father and the Son, but He is also excited to honor all those who love Them too. No wonder, then, that His precious revelations come while giving and receiving priesthood blessings or as needed by those we are assigned to lead. This includes, especially so, those times when our normal preparations are inadequate and we need nudges toward themes we would not typically develop when speaking in public. Indeed, continuous revelation seems to mean more continuous work. But come it does, particularly when our desires become subjected to what the Lord wants and after we express an openness to be taught.

Much of the revelation we receive is for the benefit of others, meaning that our Heavenly Father wants us to act on His behalf to bring about His purposes. If we expect or are seeking revelation for others within our circles of influence, we should expect to first learn about them, specifically their names. And for some in administrative callings, such proximity can bring revelatory glimpses of future assignments that others might fill as you serve them well in advance of the appointed time for their call to serve. Recognize the gifts of God in those He has asked you to lead so that you can lift their level of service.

In the meantime, we have the opportunity to mentor those seeking revelation for their own lives. Effective mentoring of another requires asking pointed questions, something that can invite the mentee to see their problem clearly and in a manner not viewed before. Questions must focus on the individual and their work or issue. Assume no responsibility for their work or problem. Describe where certain paths may lead and the value and benefits that may come from pursuing a certain course, always reinforcing the revelatory rule that information from the Holy Ghost comes most clearly when the individual seeks counsel directly from their Heavenly Father. That means giving less advice than either you or your listener may prefer at the time. Additionally, as so often is the case, encouraging others to seek God's forgiveness is the basic rule of counseling others. But when such assurances are received, we do well to also remember that the Lord will not make decisions for us but will respect our agency to choose. And then

He will confirm through the Holy Ghost. Sometimes, when working through difficult problems as a group, we might feel nudged to follow the consensus—the best information available—while being sensitive to the needs of people and waiting for the Spirit to fill in the rest.

Beyond mentoring and counseling together within councils, we also have so many opportunities for the Holy Ghost to teach us as we labor to instruct others. Praying for individuals versus just praying for our ability to teach individuals will increase our love for them and invite revelation into the classroom. Invite class members to pray to know how the Holy Ghost communicates to them individually. Some of us would do well to ask similarly if we are not clear in such matters. Indeed, involving our spouse in key decisions or teaching approaches can invite revelation into the classroom.

Within the classroom, learn to ask for differing views of opinion and learn to tolerate those views without feeling personally attacked. Revelation will guide us toward the learning we need in order to provide the service He needs us to perform. Beyond instructing others, revelation can help us discern the learning experiences the Lord has prepared and motivate us to work harder. Additionally, the Lord may let us fail for reasons other than knowing the right answer that came as a result of revelation. But He will ensure that the information provided is validated later for our benefit.

The Lord isn't limited in using only members of the Church to accomplish His purposes either. Often He creates space—with extended periods of time, vital introductions, or timely opportunities—for His purposes to be accomplished. Certain experiences provided within such space often will prove providential in shaping the path that we should walk. Revelation about the benefits of these experiences can give you confidence in the Lord's love and plan for you. Furthermore, such information will help us when we find ourselves serving and working in situations where our skills are not fully appreciated. Moreover, we may notice, upon reflection or in the moment, that vital learning experiences proximate to important assignments within the Church serve as needed clinical experiences to learn or reinforce important counsel, direction, or warnings for us or for others.

The Lord can reveal His purposes through circumstances that reduce unspoken anxiety and burdens, lift and inspire, and meet hidden or expressed needs of individuals. Also, revelation from the Holy Ghost can come to address areas of our life that, at the moment, are not our highest priority. Such information, when received, comes so it may be recorded and shared to bless others' lives.

The Holy Ghost gives us information but rarely with accompanying explanations, so we should expect revelations of impending significance in times of need but without attending instructions on how something will be done. The Lord grants these feelings to give us hope and motivate us toward action.

If we receive promptings without instruction, we can trust that in due time, the answers to why will become clear. Oftentimes the later confirmatory information is an assurance of the correctness of the course we pursued or the message we delivered. Sometimes the assurance is packaged as recognition that we share the same mind as those the Lord has called us to lead. Especially within our families or within the Lord's Church, arriving with the same mind regarding a difficult issue after much deliberative effort is spent is often indicative of revelatory influence.

Sometimes our minds and hearts just need a nudge, and the words of the scriptures do most of the work, softening our hearts, our opinions, and our attitudes without using exact words to direct the softening. No wonder we are invited to continually try "the virtue of the word of God" (Alma 31:5).

We live in a wonderful time to experience the companionship and soothing influence of the Holy Ghost. Thankfully, we have also been blessed with special forerunners who have forged a special connection with heaven through unique experiences and prolonged, consecrated service in building the Lord's kingdom. President Henry B. Eyring is such a servant and has provided us with much to reflect upon and experiment with regarding our own relationship with the third member of the Godhead.

CHAPTER SUMMARY

1. The Holy Ghost helps us fulfill our covenant obligations.

   a. The Holy Ghost speaks to our minds and hearts in common ways.

b. The Holy Ghost communicates with us in a variety of methods, with differing degrees of frequency and directness.

c. The Holy Ghost desires high-frequency communication with low directness to help us grow and learn.

2. Revelation from the Holy Ghost comes when conditions are right.

a. Revelation requires a conducive environment.
b. Revelation prefers that our spirits and bodies are clean.
c. Frequent revelation requires an attitude of seeking the Father's will.

3. The Holy Ghost gives revelation to ground and settle us in the gospel of Jesus Christ.

a. The Holy Ghost will remove fear and anxiety.
b. The Holy Ghost gives us knowledge that is expedient for us.
c. The Holy Ghost gives us an assurance that our course of life is correct.

4. The Holy Ghost's revelatory methods teach us about who He is.

a. The Holy Ghost dislikes competition.
b. The Holy Ghost values unity.
c. The Holy Ghost is patient.
d. The Holy Ghost trusts us.
e. The Holy Ghost honors the Father and the Son.
f. The Holy Ghost wants us to help others.

Reflection Questions

- What covenant obligations has the Holy Ghost helped you fulfill?
- In what ways does the Holy Ghost communicate with you?
- How has the Holy Ghost helped you understand and fulfill your covenantal obligations?

CHAPTER 10: LESSONS ON REVELATION

- What changes could you make in your life or your home to invite the Holy Ghost into your life with greater frequency?
- When was a time when the Holy Ghost helped ground or settle you in the gospel?
- How would you describe your current relationship with the Holy Ghost?
- Who do you know who would benefit from what you have learned?

Conclusion

In the spring of 1997, Elder Neal A. Maxwell addressed those assembled at general conference. His remarks were brief, as he had just emerged from treatments for the cancer that would ultimately claim his life. What was on his mind that day? One thing he stressed was the preeminence of our loving "Father-God" and His plan of redemption, which this work has shown is a reflection of His covenant with all of us, His spirit children. He said, "The redeeming presence of our loving Father-God in the universe is the grand fact pertaining to the human condition. It is the supernal truth which, along with His plan of happiness, reigns preeminent and imperial over all other realities."[156]

In addition to His praise and gratitude to our Heavenly Father, Elder Maxwell stressed gratitude and admiration for Jesus and His role in the plan of redemption in redeeming each of us. It is Jesus who bore our sins and carried our sorrows and afflictions, becoming Himself "a man of sorrows" (Isaiah 53:3). Finally, he expressed gratitude to the third member of the Godhead—the premortal covenant trio—who acts at the Savior's direction to bear witness of Him, our Father, and comfort us amidst our suffering. It is of "the Holy Ghost," said Elder Maxwell, "whom we speak less. Among his many roles I

---

156. Neal A. Maxwell, "From Whom All Blessings Flow," *Ensign*, May 1997, 12.

express my particular and personal gratitude today for the recent ways in which he has been the precious Comforter, including in the midnight moments."[157] All thanks and praise be to our righteous God, who continually gives all He has to ensure we can receive the same from Him hereafter.

Moving in His Majesty and Power

Our Heavenly Father has so structured His plan that He can be seen everywhere: in the universe, the solar system, the planetary systems, the celestial bodies, the air we breathe, our bodies, and even our very cells. We are told that all these systems—and innumerable others—"have a law given . . . for there is no space in the which there is no kingdom; and there is no kingdom in which there is no space, either a greater or a lesser kingdom" (Doctrine and Covenants 88:37). Unto all of these various systems, or kingdoms, God reigns supreme, having provided the laws to govern them. When we learn to see them for what they are, we come to see our Father "moving in his majesty and power" (Doctrine and Covenants 88:47).

All of the creation is to enable our growth and development and to glorify our Father, the Most High God. Our Father is glorified as we accept and embrace His covenant with us. He has already glorified His name through the works of Jesus (see 3 Nephi 9:15), in taking upon Himself the sins of the world (see 3 Nephi 11:11). Indeed, Jesus gave His blood that His Father might be glorified (see Doctrine and Covenants 45:3), completing His preparations of the Father's glorious plan (see Doctrine and Covenants 19:19).

Keeping the commandments of Jesus keeps us in the Father's love, which is His joy (see John 15:10), and He is continually glorified as we live His plan and become "fruitful" branches in His vineyard (see

---

157. Neal A. Maxwell, "From Whom All Blessings Flow," 12. Elder Quentin L. Cook, then serving in the Philippines Area Presidency, shared with the Quezon City Mission—where I was then serving as a full-time missionary—that the collective witness of the Holy Ghost felt by those in attendance at this time was like unto the witness of the Savior Jesus Christ felt during the last remarks of Elder Bruce R. McConkie at general conference shortly before his passing (see Bruce R. McConkie, "The Purifying Power of Gethsemane," *Ensign*, May 1985).

John 15:8). For example, when we pray to Him in the name of His Only Begotten Son (see John 14:13), He is glorified. When we let our light shine, we glorify Him (see Matthew 5:16). When we receive His covenantal offerings and receive His ordinances, including eternal marriage, "the works of the Father continue, and he glorifies himself" (Doctrine and Covenants 132:31). Indeed, the Father rejoices over generations present and past who are faithfully living the gospel of the Son (see 3 Nephi 27:30), a truth that Jesus made abundantly clear to the Nephite faithful. Keeping our covenants with Him fulfills His purpose, even His work and His glory "to bring to pass the immortality and eternal life of man" (Moses 1:39). Our Father, from the beginning, has sent angels to men and women on earth to prepare their hearts to believe in Christ and to fulfill His covenants to His children (see Moroni 7:32), and He is still hard at work. His works and words never cease (see Moses 1:4).

INVITATION

This work has attempted to expand our view of the Father's covenant with all of us from the beginning. His love and concern for us has brought us to this place—here and now—with the knowledge of His covenantal promises and plan of redemption. We know what we know and trust Him because He has taken everything into account for all of us to press forward completely and knows perfectly where we all are in His vineyard (see 3 Nephi 17:4). As one of His latter-day servants has recently testified, "Our Father's beautiful plan, even His 'fabulous' plan, is designed to bring you home, not to keep you out. . . . God is in relentless pursuit of you."[158] So trust the Father, trust His Son, and trust the Holy Ghost, who is the minister of Them both. Invite God's presence into your life more fully by making and keeping covenants with Him.

This is the path to becoming as He is. It is the path to having the Father's Spirit—His mind and His desires—dwell within us and to receiving of His glory and His fulness (see Doctrine and Covenants 93:4, 17). Through prayer and revelation from the Holy Ghost, the

---

158. Patrick Kearon "God's Intent Is to Bring You Home," *Liahona*, May 2024, 87.

Father will help you discern spirits and influences you cannot understand (see Doctrine and Covenants 50:31). He has promised that ultimately you can receive a knowledge of everything of eternal worth through the power of the Holy Ghost (see Moroni 10:5). So come and get what you said you wanted so very long ago. As Moroni encourages:

O then despise not, and wonder not, but hearken unto the words of the Lord, and ask the Father in the name of Jesus for what things soever ye shall stand in need. Doubt not, but be believing, and begin as in times of old, and come unto the Lord with all your heart, and work out your own salvation with fear and trembling before him. . . .

And may the Lord Jesus Christ grant that [your] prayers may be answered according to [your] faith; and may God the Father remember the covenant which he hath made with the house of Israel; and may he bless [you] forever, through faith on the name of Jesus Christ. Amen" (Mormon 9:27, 37).

Appendix: Four Principles of Putting On the Character of Jesus

The following lists help demonstrate the four principles of putting on the character of Jesus, as discussed in chapter 8.

Principle 1: Honor the Father with Exact Obedience to His Commandments

- Jesus was about His Father's business from a young age (Luke 2:49)
- Jesus only did what He saw His Father do (John 5:19)
- Jesus only speaks the words given to Him from the Father (John 12:49–50)
- Jesus laid down His life and took it up again at His Father's command (John 10:18)
- Jesus spoke to His disciples all the words given Him of the Father (John 15:15)

- Jesus sends His disciples into the world exactly as the Father sent Him (John 20:21)
- Jesus obeys the Father because He loves Him (John 14:31)
- Jesus finished the work assigned to Him by the Father (John 17:4)
- Jesus humbled Himself before the Father according to the flesh (2 Nephi 31:7)
- Jesus ensures that all the Father's words are recorded so they are not lost (3 Nephi 23; 24; 26)

PRINCIPLE 2: SUBJECT OUR WILL TO THE WILL OF THE FATHER, INCLUDING HIS TIMING AND EXPEDIENCY

- Jesus suffered the will of the Father in all things from the beginning (3 Nephi 11:11)
- Jesus came by the will of the Father and does His will (Doctrine and Covenants 19:24)
- Jesus could do nothing of Himself, only the will of the Father (John 5:30)
- Jesus desires that all things done on earth are according to His Father's will, as is done in heaven (Luke 11:2)
- Jesus was called the Son because He subjected His flesh to His Father's will (Mosiah 15:2)
- Jesus subjected His flesh to His Father's spirit, or will, giving Him power over death (Mosiah 15:5, 7–8)
- Jesus desired something less painful but submitted His will to the Father anyway (Mark 14:36)
- Jesus accomplished and finished the will of the Father (Doctrine and Covenants 19:2)
- Jesus promises that whosoever does the will of the Father will be His brother or sister (Matthew 12:50)
- We witness our willingness to humble ourselves according to the flesh as we keep Jesus's commandments (2 Nephi 31:13)

Principle 3: Diligently Seek Nourishment to Our Souls, Both Body and Spirit

- Do the will of the Father (Matthew 7:21)
- Worship the Father in spirit and truth (John 4:23)
- Hallow the Father's name (Luke 11:2)
- Receive the Son (Joseph Smith Translation, John 6:44)
- Confess the Son before men (Matthew 10:32–33)
- Fast discreetly (Matthew 6:17–18)
- Ask, seek, knock (Joseph Smith Translation, Matthew 7:12–17)
- Give alms in secret (Matthew 6:4)
- Honor your father and mother (Matthew 15:4)
- Bear fruit, hold up your light, and do good works (John 15:1–2; 3 Nephi 12:16; Doctrine and Covenants 58:27)
- Be unified with others when asking of the Father (Matthew 18:19)
- Pray in private and ask for what you need (Matthew 6:6–8)
- Lay up treasures in heaven (Matthew 6:20–24)
- Despise not little children (Matthew 18:10)
- Forgive men their trespasses (Matthew 6:14–15; 18:35)
- Believe in the words of Jesus's servants, the prophets (Matthew 21:28–32; Jacob 4:5)
- Treat the least of all people like a king or queen (Matthew 25:35–40)
- Love your enemies, bless those that curse you, do good to them who hate you, and pray for them who despitefully use you (Matthew 5:41–42)
- Offer a broken heart and contrite spirit, rend the veil of unbelief, and discover how the Father has fulfilled His covenant with you (Ether 4:15)
- Strive to know the Father and receive eternal life (John 17:3)
- Be as perfect as you know how, as Jesus and the Father do (Matthew 5:48; 3 Nephi 12:48; 27:27)

Principle 4: Acknowledge the Primacy of Jesus Christ in the Father's Plan

- Jesus was with the Father in the beginning (3 Nephi 9:15)
- Jesus was/is in the bosom of the Father, implying authority, connection, and unity (John 1:18; Doctrine and Covenants 76:13)
- The Father wills that the life, light, spirit, and power are sent to us through Jesus Christ (Doctrine and Covenants 50:27)
- The Father prescribes the Son's power to create and redeem (Doctrine and Covenants 76:42)
- The Father relinquished His sheep to His Son to redeem (John 10:29)
- The glory of the Only Begotten of the Father is to be full of grace and truth (Doctrine and Covenants 93:11)
- Jesus received the fulness of His Father's Spirit (Joseph Smith Translation, John 3:34)
- Jesus is called the Father because He was conceived physically by His Father in Heaven (Mosiah 15:3)
- The Father and Son have life in Themselves (John 5:26)
- Jesus received grace for grace from His Father (Doctrine and Covenants 93:12–14)
- Jesus came in His Father's name (John 5:43)
- Jesus's words were all fulfilled by the Father (Joseph Smith Translation, Matthew 19:26)
- Jesus was always heard by His Father (John 11:41)
- Jesus was sent to be lifted up to draw all men unto Him by the power of the Father (3 Nephi 27:14–15)
- The Father glorified Jesus by giving Him power over the spirits of all men, similar to Him giving power over their flesh, in advance of the Atonement (John 17:1–2)
- Jesus was always with His Father (John 16:32), until the time of His Atonement when the Father was hidden from Him and Jesus felt forsaken (Matthew 27:46; Mark 15:34)
- Jesus is our Advocate with the Father (Doctrine and Covenants 29:5; 32:3; 45:2)

- Jesus kept His Father's commandments and abode in His love, or His joy (John 15:10)
- You cannot follow Jesus without keeping the Father's commandments given to Jesus (2 Nephi 31:10)
- No one can come unto Christ except He does the will of the Father (Joseph Smith Translation, John 6:65)

About the Author

Joshua L. Savage earned his doctorate from the University of Southern California. He currently works for a Fortune 50 company as a principal consultant, helping leaders transform their organizations by thinking differently.

Dr. Savage is the author of four books, including the previous titles *Renewing Your Relationship with Jesus* and *Divine Identity* with Cedar Fort Publishing. Dr. Savage served a mission in the Philippines Quezon City Mission. He and his wife, Jennifer Gardner Savage, are the parents of four children and currently reside in Gilbert, Arizona.